CONTENTS

Introduction 5

Deadly Dark Ages 7

Murky Middle Ages 13

The Hundred Years War that wasn't 42

Cruel crimes 55

Revolting France 65

Kurious kings 87

Quirky queens and wicked women 103

Savage seventeenth century 111

Awful for animals 119

Evil eighteenth century 128

Nasty nineteenth century 162

Epilogue 174

Introduction

Some people in history have been revolting. They revolt against anything. They revolt against their rulers, they revolt against paying taxes, they revolt against paying too much for food.

You must know how those rebels feel – you probably revolt against eating Brussels sprouts, or too much homework, or washing your dad's car for 20p.

There's nothing wrong with a good revolt. Sometimes it's the only way to change things. If it hadn't been for rebels you might not be reading this book ... you might be a slave in some rich person's house, working 23 hours a day and paid in mouse droppings. (Or, if you're really lucky, something a bit more filling ... like rat droppings.)

But some countries seem to have been better at revolutions than others. Take France. They probably had the best revolution of all time. In 1789 they had a revolution that got rid of kings and lords in a big way. It was real...

How did the French get to be so good at revolting? Simple. They got lots and lots of practice. Through the years they had peasant revolts, religious revolts and student revolts – princes revolted against their fathers and lords against their kings.

And the French didn't mess about when they revolted. There was no going up to a lord and saying…

No. The French tortured, burned, executed, cut, gouged, hacked and sliced their way through dozens of revolutions. They all failed, of course, until in 1789 the people finally got it right and got rid of their king soon after.

Then they changed their minds and decided they liked kings after all – for a while.

And when they weren't rebelling they were eating weird food, being killed or cured by dreadful doctors, fighting against the English (their favourite foe), or fighting each other in deadly duels. The French could be foul, but you could never accuse them of being boring.

The history of the revolting French is pretty horrible, of course. Horrible history, in fact. But no one has ever put all these horrible French facts into one book. Until now, that is. Read on…

Deadly Dark Ages

In the Dark Ages 'France' was the land of the 'Franks'. A tough bunch of people who came from the north of Europe and booted everybody else out – even the Romans. Here's roughly how they did it...

AD **200s** The Franks are a group of people living by the Baltic Sea – which is a bit chilly – in a place called Pomerania – which is a bit of a silly name. They move south and settle on the River Rhine, outside the Roman Empire.

287 This is the first we hear of a Frankish leader – Genobaud – when the Romans beat him in battle. Those fearsome Franks will be back...

300s The Franks cross the Rhine and spread into part of the Roman Empire in an area called Gaul – now northern France and western Germany. The western Franks will become 'French' and the Eastern Franks 'German'.

355 A Frank, Silvanus, becomes emperor of Rome ... for 28 days. Then he sets off for church and is hacked to pieces by his enemies.

388 The Franks, led by Marcomeres and Sunno, cross the frontier to attack the Romans in Gaul. The Franks then pretend to run away – the rotten Romans follow them ... into a trap. The Romans are massacred – but Sunno is killed. By his own men, the Franks. Franks a lot, mates.

476 Roman Emperor Romulus Augustulus is overthrown and the Romans become too weak to rule Gaul. The Franks simply rule themselves with their own kings. Of course just because these kings are all Franks doesn't mean they'll live happily ever together. Oh, no. They will squabble for hundreds of years to be top poodle.

507 Crafty but cruel Clovis rules in Gaul. He wipes out the Franks back in Germany, then begins to wipe out his own family. He complains he is lonely … and invites his surviving relatives to join him. They say no. Wonder why?

511 Clovis dies and France is split between his four sons. They are called the Merovingian kings.

732 Arabs raid southern France. Frank hero, Charles Martel, leads a lot of peasants to a great victory. Charles's family, the Carolingian kings, replace the Merovingian kings.

799 Carolingian king Charlemagne rescues the Pope from his enemies. His reward is to be made 'Emperor' of France, Germany and Northern Italy. Some power. (In 1254 the Germans will call this ruler 'Holy Roman Emperor'.)

810 The fearless Franks come up against a new enemy – the Vikings. But the Viking King Godfred is assassinated so France is spared … for a while. Charlemagne dies in 814 and the Franks aren't so strong now – watch out!

885 A huge Viking army attacks Paris – defenders pour boiling oil, wax and tar on the Viking noddles. Ouch. After a year's siege the French pay the Vikings to go away. So, of course, they'll be back.

923 Robert the rebel has nicked the throne from King Charles of France. This year Charles kills him and nicks it back. What a Charley.

Cruel Clovis

Clovis was a cruel and crafty Frankish king. If someone upset him he didn't lose his cool. He waited and plotted … then struck viciously. The story of Clovis and the stroppy soldier is a good example.

Chopper Charlemagne

French King Charlemagne was a great warrior and he made the people he clobbered, like the Saxons, follow the Christian religion – even if he had to kill them to do it! In 788 he had 4,500 Saxon prisoners beheaded – in one day. The French choppers must have been exhausted. (Charlemagne fought the Saxons for 33 years – and started a French fashion for l-o-n-g wars.)

Charlemagne had so much power there were bound to be people who wanted to take it from him. Champion Charlie wasn't easy to chop, though several tried. Charlemagne's son, Pepin, a handsome hunchback, plotted with Frankish lords to kill Charlemagne. Pepin's plot was discovered. He had his head shaved and was sent off to be a monk. Some of Pepin's mates were less lucky – they were banished after having their eyes put out.

PICK UP PEPIN'S PERFECTLY PUTRID PALS AND PLUCK THEIR PUPILS!

Plucking eyes was a popular pastime. Charlemagne's big buddy was Pope Leo III. Jealous enemies of the Pope attacked Leo III in the street in 799. A gang of armed men tried to rip out the Pope's eyes and his tongue. But they didn't kill him, and Leo's eyes and tongue recovered! (It is said he healed because he was a saint!)

Charlemagne sent an army to help Leo and the grateful Pope crowned Charlemagne 'Holy Roman Emperor'.

When Charlemagne was crowned Emperor he acted shocked. He said…

If I'd known the Pope was going to crown me I'd never have come into the church!

Hmmm! A likely story.

Did you know…?
Charlemagne had a great bridge built over the River Rhine at Mayence. The bridge caught fire in 813 and burned to ashes. It was a 'bad sign' the people said. Another 'bad sign' was a black spot seen on the sun. Later a ball of fire fell from the sky and spooked Charlemagne's horse so it threw him off. There were earthquakes, lightning strikes, and thunderbolts that smashed houses and churches. What did these 'bad signs' mean? Charlemagne was going to die – and he did in 814!

Murky Middle Ages

The Middle Ages (from around 1000 to around 1500) were hugely horrible. Cruelty and crime, plague and pain, battles and blood, wars and witchcraft, terror and torture, robber bands[1] and riots. Especially riots. This was the age when the peasants started to fight back against the lords.

France was made up of large regions ruled by powerful dukes. The dukes ruled with their knights in armour and only obeyed the King of France when it suited them. Sometimes peasants revolted against their dukes – and sometimes the dukes revolted against the king. Sometimes religious rebels revolted against the Catholic Church. It was just a revolting time to be alive.

1033 French people panic. It is 1,000 years since the death of Christ and they think the world is going to end. Storms destroy the crops. Many starve. It *is* the end of the world for them.
1106 Emperor Henry IV, the Holy Roman Emperor, defeats his rebel son ... then dies. The son becomes Henry V. If Henry V had waited for dad to die he could have saved all the fighting.
1208 Pope Innocent III calls for a new Crusade against the people of south-west France – Languedoc. What had they done? Argued with the Catholic Church's beliefs – they are 'heretics'.
1212 Stephen of Cloyes, a 12–year-old shepherd boy, leads the Children's Crusade to the Holy

---

1 Robber bands roamed the roads to rob the rich. These are not to be confused with *rubber* bands that are only useful at flicking at teachers.

Land – helped by William the Pig (honest!). Most of the young crusaders end up sold as slaves or dying of disease.

1231 The Catholic Church's 'Inquisition' is formed to seek out and destroy heretics – they will go on to terrorize Europe for hundreds of years to come with terrible tortures and brutal burnings.

1244 Massacre at Montségur. Non-Catholics killed. Meanwhile King Louis IX is put in his coffin ready for burial. Suddenly he sits up and recovers. He will reign another 26 years.

1309 King Philip IV has to hide in a Paris temple when a mob sets out to kill him. Just one of many revolutions against French kings.

1328 Revolting peasants in northern France – peasant army destroyed and their leader executed horribly.

1337 The Hundred Years War starts between France and England when Edward III of England says, 'I am King of France.' and the French say, 'Oh no you're not.'

1348 The 'Black Death' arrives in France, a dreadful plague that gives you purple spots and turns you smelly and then probably kills you.

1431 French heroine Joan of Arc is rewarded for leading France to victories against the evil English – she is burned as a witch.

1440 Now Joan's friend, French Lord Gilles de Rais, is executed for killing kids.

1453 Lord Talbot's English army defeated by French cannon at Castillon. The Hundred Years War started with victories for English archers. It ends with a French archer, Michael Perunin, giving Talbot the chop with a battle-axe.

1572 St Bartholomew's Day Massacre. Catholic King Charles IX lures his enemies to Paris. He invites them to his sister's wedding – then has them killed. Some say 27,000 died in the massacre.

Cruelty to Cathars

In Languedoc in south-west France the people began to object to the way the Catholic Church was run. The Languedoc rebels were called 'Cathars'.

Why? Many history books will tell you 'Cathars' means 'pure ones'. *Horrible Histories* can tell you it comes from German words meaning 'cat worshippers'. That's because their Catholic enemies said that a Cathar had to kiss the bum of a black cat.

15

So what did the Cathars call themselves? Was it…
a) Ex-Christians
b) Awkward Christians
c) Good Christians?

Answer: c) They followed the teachings of Jesus Christ, so they were *Christians*. They just didn't agree with the way the Christian *Church* was run.

Deadly differences

The head of the Catholic Church, Pope Innocent III, was upset. The Cathars did not agree with the Church on some important matters…

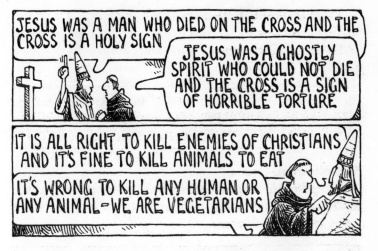

The Pope couldn't have people going around saying things like that. He'd be out of a job in no time. Anyone who didn't follow the Catholic Church was a 'heretic' and often the punishment for heretics was to be burned alive.

Did you know…?

When the Pope moved in the 1300s from Rome to France, the Pope's new palace at Avignon had two whole floors of terrific toilets! They had stone seats (a bit cold in winter) and emptied into pits below the ground. A stream was diverted to wash the sewage away.

But the people in the town of Avignon, outside the palace, suffered. They were crowded out with the Pope's followers and there weren't enough toilets to go round. The smell in summer made the townfolk ill.

Cathar cwiz

Cathars and cruelty seemed to go together. Can you work out which of these cruel Cathar facts are true?

1 The Pope's Crusaders are about to attack the town of Beziers in 1209. The soldiers ask monk Arnold Amaury, 'How do we tell the difference between good Catholics and wicked Cathars?' What does Amaury answer?

a) 'Kill them all. God will tell the difference when they get to heaven.'

b) 'Capture them all and torture them to get the truth.'

c) 'The Catholics will be able to recite the Lord's Prayer, the Cathars can't.'

2 The Cathars could be a bit rough too. The Catholics said the Cathars captured a Catholic priest and did what?

a) Made the priest kiss a black cat's bum.

b) Made a black cat kiss the priest's bum.

c) Chopped him into pieces.

3 The most ruthless soldiers were the foot soldiers who fought in the Crusade for money – 'routiers'. What were routiers said to do for fun?

a) Roast live cats over a fire.

b) Roast live children over a fire.

c) Roast chestnuts over a fire.

4 Simon de Montfort was leader of the Crusade and his job was to persuade the Cathars to become Catholics. How did he do this in the Bram region of France?

a) He sent priests in to preach to them 48 hours non-stop.

b) He said, 'Do you want to be a Catholic with a head or a Cathar without a head?'

c) He pulled out the eyes of the Cathars and sliced off their noses and lips.

5 Simon de Montfort moved on to Minerve in June 1210 and captured lots of Cathars. When 140 Cathars refused to become Catholics, what did Simon de M do to them?

a) Burned them on one big bonfire.

b) Smacked them on the wrist and told them the Pope would be angry with them.

c) Told them, 'I forgive you.'

6 The Lady of Lavaur sheltered 400 Cathars and refused to give them up to de Montfort. When she was captured in May 1211 how did de Montfort treat her?

a) Like a lady. But he forced her to go into a nunnery.

b) Like a dog. He had her thrown down a well and stones piled on top of her.

c) Like a man. He had her nose and ears cut off.

19

7 By 1216 the Cathars were fighting back. When they captured Catholic soldiers they sometimes cut off their feet and used them to what?

a) Throw at the Catholic enemies.

b) Keep their slippers warm at the end of a hard day's killing.

c) Kick around like a football game – except it was a foot-foot game of course.

8 Simon de Montfort tried to attack Toulouse in 1217 but was killed by a rock on the head. What were his last words after he was hit by the rock?

a) 'Toulouse. Toulouse, I thought I had nothing to lose.'

b) 'Oi. Who threw that rock?'

c) '*Splat.*'

9 Simon's great enemy, the Count of Toulouse, died of old age in 1222. What happened to his body?

a) It was buried at sea.

b) It was buried at the spot where Simon de Montfort was splattered.

c) It wasn't buried and was eaten by rats.

10 The King of France took over the war against the Cathars – and failed. Finally the Pope sent in men to seek out, torture and burn Cathars. Who were these torturers?

a) Soldiers.

b) Monks.

c) School teachers.

Answers:

1a) This idea is still tried by some school football teams – 'If it moves – kick it.' (Of course all readers of *Horrible Histories* play that way.) The soldiers did what they were told and massacred everyone, from babies and women to priests. Maybe the monk didn't say those exact words – but the soldiers did it anyway. Twenty thousand died.

2c) The story may not be true, just a lie made up by the Catholics to make the Cathars look evil. But people *believed* it. Some people will believe anything.

3b) The routiers were more terrifying than the knights. They were badly armed and many didn't even have shoes. But they were vicious and showed little mercy. They made good Crusaders because they were afraid of nothing – just like *Horrible Histories* readers.

4c) One man was left with one eye. The one–eyed man was given the job of leading his blind mates to the next fortress as a warning: 'Mess with Simon and you'll never see (or smell) your feet again.' Simon de M's excuse for the cruelty was that the Cathars had done the same to two Catholic knights. Other knights had their skin ripped off while they were alive and ordinary soldiers often had hands or feet chopped off if they were lucky – if they were unlucky they were simply chopped into pieces.

ARE YOU GIVING ME LIP? HA HA!

'ERY 'UNNY

5a) The Cathars were burned. Some witnesses said the Cathars were so happy to die the Catholics didn't have to throw them on the bonfire – they threw themselves on.

Burning was going to be a popular way of killing off Cathars.

6b) The lady died horribly but not as horribly as some of her knights. Eighty of them were lined up to be hanged all at once. But the weight was too great and the hanging beam collapsed. They had their throats cut instead. The captured Cathars were burned.

7a) The prisoners were hanged or chopped up but using feet as missiles was nasty.

Toe – tow … geddit? Oh, never mind.

8c) Simon de Montfort said nothing because his head was caved in. They said that women and girls fired the stone that killed him. A historian of the time said:

The stone hit Count Simon on his steel helmet in such a way that his eyeballs, brains, teeth, skull and jawbone all flew into pieces. He fell down upon the ground stark dead, blackened and bloody.

Now that's what you call 'out for the count'.

9c) The Count of Toulouse had fought against the Catholic Church – so the Catholic Church said, 'Right. We refuse to bury you in a Catholic churchyard. Serves you right.' So the body was left in a coffin in a garden next to the churchyard where it rotted and was nibbled by rats. The bones were scattered.

WHY AREN'T THESE BONES JOINED TOGETHER?

MAYBE THEY'RE TOO LOOSE

All right … no more Toulouse – to lose – too loose jokes. Not even the one about the family with an upstairs toilet and a downstairs toilet who were known as the two loos family…

10b) The monks went in with the help of soldiers and tortured people to confess – or betray friends who were Cathars. They were known as the Inquisition. If you didn't confess you were tortured till you did confess – if you did confess you were burned. The Cathars last stand was in 1244 at their fortress of Montségur. They were finally captured and given a choice – become a Catholic or burn: 220 men and women chose to burn. They died together in one huge fire. The Catholic Church had 'won' the war – but lost a lot of friends and a lot of respect. If the Cathars never recovered from the massacre at Montségur, then neither did the Catholic Church.

Deadly doctors and disgusting diseases

French doctors, like most other doctors in the Middle Ages, used a mixture of magic, killer cures and real cures. They never quite knew which was which, of course. Here are a few of the most peculiar. Match the illness to the cure – but it doesn't matter if you get it wrong, because it probably wouldn't work anyway.

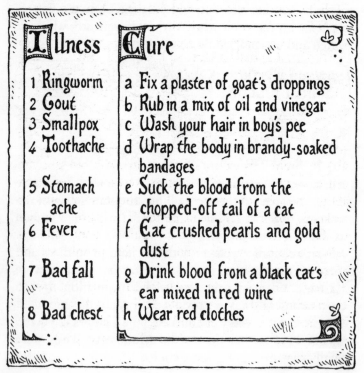

Illness

1 Ringworm
2 Gout
3 Smallpox
4 Toothache
5 Stomach ache
6 Fever
7 Bad fall
8 Bad chest

Cure

a Fix a plaster of goat's droppings
b Rub in a mix of oil and vinegar
c Wash your hair in boy's pee
d Wrap the body in brandy-soaked bandages
e Suck the blood from the chopped-off tail of a cat
f Eat crushed pearls and gold dust
g Drink blood from a black cat's ear mixed in red wine
h Wear red clothes

Answers:

1c) Ringworm is a sort of fungus that makes itchy red rings – usually on your scalp. It has to be treated with fungus killers. Boy's pee might not kill the fungus – but it would give it a bit of a nasty shock.

2a) Gout is caused by crystals in your blood that stop your blood flowing freely. It is very painful at the point where the crystals gather – often in the foot. Goat's droppings (mixed with honey) may give you a warm and soothing plaster. It will also make your feet smell nearly as bad as they do now.

3h) Smallpox is a virus like flu. But it makes you hot and sick and spotty. The spots leave scars that make your face look like the surface of the moon. The cure was wearing red clothes, and sitting in a room with daylight coming through red curtains. A waste of red cloth for all the good it will do you.

4b) It might take some of the pain away but not the cause – rotten teeth. But doctors weren't too bothered about 'curing' the patient. The doctor's job was to make the patient feel a bit better. The 'cure' was left to God. (Let's hope God's waiting room isn't as crowded as our waiting rooms or sick people will be there a l-o-n-g time.)

5f) You need to be pretty rich for this, but that's what the wealthy Duke of Berry ate. It didn't kill him – but it made his peasants poor and angry. To know they were paying taxes just so he could swallow their gold made them revolt.

6d) The doctor prescribed this for the vicious Charles of Navarre. The idea was that he would sweat till the fever left him. But he went too near fire. Ever seen a Christmas pudding soaked in brandy? Hold a match to it and what happens? Pow. It burns. Charles caught fire when a servant leaned too close with a candle and, because he was sewn into the bandages, couldn't escape. Char-grilled Charlie died after two weeks of agony.

7e) Chopping off a cat's tail is cruel to the cat. But drinking blood from that tail is better than another cure for stomach ache – you have to drink wine mixed with pussy-cat poo! Phew!

8g) Cats figured in a lot of cures because they were said to be magical with powers of witchcraft. To cure a field full of weeds just bury a cat alive in the field. Nasty. And to make yourself invisible eat the raw brain of a cat while it is still warm.

Did you know…?

In 1635 the French banned sales of tobacco. Good idea? The trouble was they said you could still get it from your doctor if he said you needed it to cure you. (Cure you of what? Life?) Tobacco had been brought to France by Mr Nicot in the 1500s.

Foul fleece

Louis XVI's daughter-in-law gave birth to a child on a scorching hot day and felt ill. The doctor came up with a curious cure for her. What was it? Here's a clue … she survived…

a) He had 50 frogs killed in her bedroom, made into a soup and fed to her.

b) He had a sheep killed and skinned in her bedroom then had her wrapped in the bleeding skin.

c) He had a peacock killed in her bedroom and used its tail feathers as a huge fan to keep her cool.

Answer: **b)** The sheep skin cure made her better — well, you'd pretend to be better if someone wrapped a smelly sheep fleece round you, wouldn't you? She wanted to nod off but the doctor forced her to stay awake for hours. Finally he had her sealed up in the room, in the heat, for nine days without even a candle for light. And you thought your doctor was cruel?

Disgusting disease

In 1494 Charles VIII invaded Italy. He arrived at Naples with his army and sent messengers to demand the city surrendered… The messengers came back with their ears and noses cut off!

But that trip to Italy got rid of more noses than just those messengers'. The French soldiers returned home with a disease. It ate away at the roof of the mouth, then the lips, the nose and the eyes.

Priests and doctors argued over the cause…

God or worms (or even germs), the result was often death.

Handy doctor

Paris Doctors' Monthly 1539

The top army doc, Ambroise Paré, has come up with a sensational new treatment for soldiers who lose arms and legs in battle. He makes new mechanical body bits for them!

Paré's fake hands have pen holders built into them and some of them have fingers that move with the help of little cogs, like a clock. This fabulous Frenchman will even fit you with false teeth or a false eye!

Of course Ambroise has become famous for his treatment of battle wounds. Old surgeons used boiling oil to pour into gunshot wounds – Ambroise uses a mixture of egg yolk, rose oil and turpentine. 'Far less painful ... and it works better,' one victim said happily.

And when soldiers had an arm or leg amputated in battle, the wound used to be 'sealed' with red-hot irons. Ouch! But our caring Ambroise has started tying the blood vessels to stop the bleeding.

With docs like Ambroise Paré around it's almost a pleasure to get shot for France.

It could have been worse

The Duchess of Orleans lived at Versailles Palace in the days of Louis XIV. She had been born in Germany and happily took the awful French treatments because there were worse cures in Germany at that time. She wrote letters home and said...

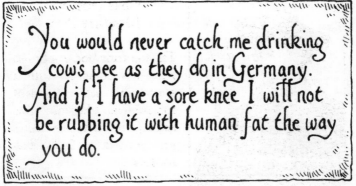

You would never catch me drinking cow's pee as they do in Germany. And if I have a sore knee I will not be rubbing it with human fat the way you do.

Human fat? From a dead human, I guess.

Did you know…?

Doctors believed in cutting a patient and letting out blood. Louis XIII had blood let out 47 times in one month. It's a wonder he had any left.

Funny bones

When the doctors failed to save your life, and you died, your bones didn't get a lot of peace in Paris in the 1400s. Most corpses were buried in the Cemetery of the Innocents.

This cheerful place had paintings on the walls – paintings of Death.

Mr Death became fashionable in a street theatre performance called the 'Danse Macabre' (the Gruesome Dance). In the play there were 15 pairs of people from Pope and Emperor down to peasant and child. They stepped forward and said something like…

With the dead folk of this land.
Popes and peasants, brave knights too,
One day Death will swallow you.
We are dead, our corpses stink,
We are here to make you think;
When you're dead, your bodies rot,
All your gold's worth not a jot.
Only good deeds save your soul
When you fall in Death's dark hole.

Charming, eh? But back to the Cemetery of the Innocents.

Your corpse would be taken to the graveyard but, if you were seriously rich, you could be buried in your own little bone-house at the cemetery.

The poor were put under the ground ... but just for a while. The cemetery was so crowded the old bones were dug up to make room for fresh ones. Skulls and bones were left lying around to remind people – like the Danse Macabre – 'One day you'll be like this.'

And the people of Paris rather liked this in the 1400s. Shops sprang up in the cemetery, selling books and clothes, cakes and ribbons. And people came to see the Danse Macabre performed or listen to preachers.

If T-shirts had been invented in those days they'd have been sold in the cemetery and probably said something like:

The cemetery closed in 1786 and it was reckoned there were two million skeletons there. They were dumped in a quarry.

Quick quiz

How horrible are you? Try this foul French quiz and find out if you could have been as nasty as the horrible historical people were. The more you score the nastier your twisted mind is.

Score 10 and you can wear a badge that says:

Score 7, 8 or 9 and you can have this one:

Score 4, 5 or 6 and you can wear this:

Score 1, 2 or 3 and wear this badge:

Score 0 and wear this:

1 In 1303 the Pope in Italy was angry because the French King was taxing priests in France. How would you sort out the 85-year-old Pope?
a) Kidnap him.
b) Stick pins in the priests.
c) Pinch all the prayer books from the churches.

2 King Jean II (1319–64) had a painter Girard D'Orleans working for him. As King Jean's painter what job would you like to do?
a) Paint King Jean's face.
b) Paint King Jean's toilet paper.
c) Paint King Jean's toilet seats.

3 In 1360 Captain Ringois led a sea raid on England and was captured. All he had to do was say he'd obey the King of England and he'd go free. He refused. What would you do rather than obey?
a) Jump off a cliff to your death.
b) Jump over your prison wall to freedom.
c) Jump on a jailer's head to escape.

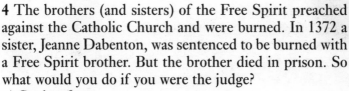

4 The brothers (and sisters) of the Free Spirit preached against the Catholic Church and were burned. In 1372 a sister, Jeanne Dabenton, was sentenced to be burned with a Free Spirit brother. But the brother died in prison. So what would you do if you were the judge?
a) Set her free.
b) Burned her anyway.
c) Burned her along with her friend's corpse.

5 A lady saw her husband beheaded by French King Philip VI. What would you do with your dead husband's head?
a) Take it home and show it to your son.
b) Bury it.
c) Pickle it and put it in the family museum.

6 Young King Charles VI had a feast after his coronation. The greatest honour was to sit next to Charles. How would you make sure you got that seat?
a) Leave the coronation early and get to the feast hall first.
b) Bribe the chief servant to put a reserved notice on the seat for you.
c) Push anyone else out of the way if they get there first—a bit like musical chairs.

7 In the 1370s one-eyed Olivier de Clisson was known as 'The Butcher'. What would you do to get a nickname like that?
a) Sell meat.
b) Become a soldier who hacks off enemy arms and legs during a battle.
c) Become a circus performer who eats live crocodiles in his act.

8 In the Middle Ages French parents and kids often shared a big bed. But it was against the law to take a baby under 12 months into your bed. This law stopped parents making an excuse. Which excuse?
a) 'I'm late for work because baby cried all night.'
b) 'Baby died because Dad rolled on top of him.'
c) 'I can't go to church because baby pooed on me in the night.'

9 In 1638 the French general, Duke de la Valette, lost a battle and ran away to England. If you were French King Louis XIII what would you do?
a) Send him a nasty letter calling Valette a cowardy custard.
b) Have Valette brought back from England and punch him on the nose.
c) Have a dummy made of Valette and have the dummy's head chopped off.

10 In 1815 a group of women were walking in Paris when two men upset them. What would you do to the men?
a) Beat them with your knickers till they run off.
b) Beat them with your shoes till they are knocked out.
c) Beat them with your umbrellas till they are dead.

Answers:
1a) The Pope was 85 when a French gang kidnapped him from his holiday home near Rome. The local people set the Pope free ... but the shock killed the old man. The next Pope was French – and he was too scared to go to Rome to rule from the Pope's palace. 'The Italians will get their revenge on me,' he argued. So the Pope stayed in France (in Avignon) and that's where the Popes lived for the rest of the century.
2c) Would you enjoy painting toilet seats? A bit of a bum job really. And what if someone sat on your painting before it had dried? They'd be walking around with your painting on their backside. France is famous for its art gallery the Louvre – maybe it should have one called the Loo-seat.

3a) Ringois was thrown into a miserable dungeon and threatened with death. He refused to give in. In the end he was taken to the cliffs of Dover and told, 'Obey or jump onto those rocks below.' He jumped.

4c) Well, it's nice to have a bit of company when you're being burned, isn't it? Someone to chat to, have one last joke with.

5a) Lady de Clisson took her husband's head home to Brittany and showed it to her seven-year-old son, Olivier. She made him swear that he would grow up to become a knight and fight the French. Which he did. But later de Clisson also became the French King, Charles V's, 'Constable' – in charge of law and order for France! He made lots of money and lots of enemies.

6c) The Duke of Anjou and the Duke of Burgundy *both* thought they should sit next to the new king. They scrambled and scrapped for the seat like two kids. The King's council said, 'Burgundy should have it.' Anjou said, 'I'm having it any way,' and sat down. He had to be dragged off. Still it turned out to be quite a party. Three great lords rode on horses to serve the 12-year-old King. In the streets fountains ran with water, milk and wine.

7b) When in battle, Olivier used a huge double-edged battle-axe that was said to kill everyone it struck. He lost an eye but it didn't stop him flattening Frenchmen. In 1369 he turned back to fight for the French. One of his nastiest acts was to capture 15 Englishmen and have them locked up. He then ordered that they should be released – one at a time. As each happy prisoner stepped out Olivier whacked off his head with a single stroke of his war axe. So 15 swishes, 15 happy heads rolled.

One night his enemies plotted to kill him. As Clisson rode through the streets of Paris a gang of 40 armed men attacked the Constable and his eight guards. Clisson was armed with just a dagger. The attackers had swords and hacked Clisson to the ground and kept chopping till he fell through the door of a baker shop where the baker dragged him inside. The attackers rode off leaving Clisson with 60 sword cuts. He survived.

8b) An extra baby in the family could mean the rest went hungry. So some parents smothered their babies. They gave the excuse that the baby shared their bed and it was smothered by accident. The Church passed a law saying, 'No babies in bed, then.' It probably didn't stop the babies having other 'accidents'. Be warned. Don't start sharing a bed with your parents. You may choke on the smell of Dad's socks.

9c) Sounds a bit daft – executing a dummy when you can't get your hands on the real criminal. But that's what the British people have done for hundreds of years, thousands of times, with Guy Fawkes dummies on 5 November.

10c) Paris umbrellas used by Paris women as weapons. Deadly. The women were supporters of the King. The men were supporters of the King's enemy, Napoleon. When the men shouted 'Long live Napoleon!' the women didn't argue. They just murdered the men. Ouch.

Score
So how did you score? Even if you scored 11 out of 10 you still couldn't be as horrible as some French during the murky Middle Ages.

Woe for women

Women have been badly treated in every age of history everywhere in the world. Medieval France is no different from the rest. Here are just a few foul facts...

1 In the 1300s women plucked their eyebrows and the hair on the front of their heads (to give them a high forehead). Churchmen hated this fashion – 'If God wants you to have bushy eyebrows then you should have bushy eyebrows.' They ranted, 'The punishment is waiting for you in Hell. For every hair you've pulled out, a devil will push a red-hot needle in its place.'

DAD, IF GOD WANTS YOU TO HAVE A BUSHY CHIN THEN YOU SHOULD HAVE A BUSHY CHIN

2 A writer, Menagier of Paris, wrote a list of 'rules' for women to obey in the 1350s. They were the usual things men have used to bully women for thousands of years...

A wife should never answer back
A husband's wishes are more important than a wife's wishes
A wife should advise, but never nag

Menagier probably got his own way because his wife was just 15 years old.

3 French men in the Middle Ages married girls as young as 12 so it's no wonder they could bully them so easily. A man called La Tour Landry described how a wife shouted at her husband in public. Her husband...

a) smashed her in the face with his fist

b) kicked her in the face and broke her nose.

Her face was so badly damaged, Landry said, she never showed herself in public again. Was Tour shocked by this wife-beater? No. He said:

This was what the woman deserved for using bad language to her husband.

4 In 1379 the English Earl of Arundel planned an invasion of France and his soldiers took some women along for company. Awful Arundel set off in December, which is barmy because it's a stormy time of year. The English ships were hit by the storms and needed to lose some weight if they were going to stay afloat. What did the English throw overboard? You guessed it – the women.

You will be pleased to know nasty Arundel beat up the pilot who was guiding them. Without a guide the ships soon smashed into rocks and sank. Arundel and his 25 ships went to the bottom of the sea. Only seven men survived.

5 In 1419 the English invaders were destroying Northern France and the peasants were starving. One peasant woman kept a supply of meat. It was soaked in salt water to stop it going rotten. It would last her a couple of months. But where had she got that meat?

a) She stole it from the English army by disguising herself as an army cook.

b) She killed her two children.

c) She killed a passing elephant.

Answer: **b)** Don't tell your parents (or your teachers) that kids make a tasty snack or they might decide to munch you instead of a bag of crisps. (Parents and teachers, of course, should NEVER be allowed to read a *Horrible Histories* book.)

Did you know…?

It wasn't only the women who starved in the Middle Ages. Even the wolves had a rough time. The starving animals dug up corpses from graveyards to feed themselves. Some even swam the River Seine to prey on the people of Paris. Which probably led to the ancient *Horrible Histories* joke…

The Hundred Years War that wasn't

England and France fought 'The Hundred Years War' from 1337–1453 … and if you're any good at sums you'll know that's 116 years! And they weren't fighting very much during those 116 years either. Just the odd invasion from England, a lot of time arguing and some of the time being quite friendly. Not 100 years … and not much war.

Edward III of England was the nephew of Charles IV of France – so, he said, 'If my uncle was king of France then I should be too.'

The French had different ideas and different French kings said, 'Push off, Ed.' Not a very big argument but enough to give us some nice horrible history moments. Here are a few…

1 Battling Blois

In the 1340s Charles of Blois was a leading French fighter. He was a very religious man and, for his religion…

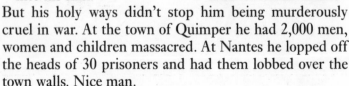

OUR HERO

- He wore clothing that was never washed, even when it was crawling with lice. Underneath he had a shirt of rough horse-hair.
- He put pebbles in his shoes.
- He slept on straw on the floor next to his wife's comfy bed.
- He wore knotted cords round his body, so tight the knots dug into his skin.

But his holy ways didn't stop him being murderously cruel in war. At the town of Quimper he had 2,000 men, women and children massacred. At Nantes he lopped off the heads of 30 prisoners and had them lobbed over the town walls. Nice man.

2 The savage sixty

In 1351 two knights from Brittany, northern France, decided to fight a duel. Robert supported the French king and Bramborough supported the English king.

When their men heard about the duel they all wanted to join in. The two knights decided to make it a 30-a-side competition. (A bit like two English rugby teams against two French rugby teams with a licence to kill.)

The English and French nations were thrilled at the idea. If they'd had newspapers in those days then 'The Combat of the Thirty' would have been front page news – or at least back-page sport headlines.

BRITTANY BUGLE  WIN A PIG — only 1 franc

27 March 1351

I'M ALL RIGHT JACQUES

The Combat of the Thirty is over and all 60 knights have been wounded. But it's mostly English-lovers' blood that is scattered over our fine French fields.

First the 60 men prayed together and then they played together. The two teams of 30 kicked off on time. They were armed with swords, bear spears, daggers and axes and it was England who scored first. After a while it was 4–2 to England as four French lay dead on the field of play to two English.

Sir Owen brought down in the penalty area.

43

Half time couldn't come quickly enough for French captain Robert. He called to the English striker, Bramborough, 'Can we stop for a drink?'

Battling English defender Geoffrey Bouays called back, 'Drink your own blood!'

If the first half belonged to the English then the second half was all France. They scored time and again till Bramborough and eight of his team lay dead on the field. Down to 21 men, the surrounded English surrendered. They will be held prisoner now till their family pay the ransom.

It was a great victory for France in this knock-out competition. Robert's super survivors will be hailed as heroes. Bramborough will be relegated to the grave while his knights suffer the agony of penalties.

Le Blanc with a stunning header

The battle decided nothing. It was just an excuse for a fight. Yet, more than 20 years later, the French fighters were remembered as heroes and were still getting a free nosh at King Charles V's table.

The French and English knights loved to believe this was the noble way to do battle. Maybe it was. But they still spent most of their time burning towns, destroying crops, stealing cattle and murdering unarmed peasants.

All the Combat of the Thirty really gave us was that great war cry: 'Drink your blood and your thirst will pass.' Try that next time your friend tries to scrounge your can of Coke.

3 Chopped Charlie

The Hundred Years War wasn't all about brave battlers. There were plenty of cut-throat cowards too. And it was often Frenchmen cutting the throats of other Frenchmen.

Charles d'Espagne became King Jean II's favourite and the jealous King of Navarre sent his brother, Philip, to give Charles d'Espagne the chop.

In January 1354 Philip's men arrived at Charlie's castle at night. Charlie was asleep and they dragged him from his bed. Most people in those days slept without any clothes; in January he must have been a chilly Charlie. Instead of facing his enemy bravely, Charlie's chat went something like this:

A Murderous Meeting

Philip stands over Charles while Philip's men hold his arms and force him to his knees.

Charles: Philip, my friend. You don't want to hurt me. Why are you holding that sword to my throat?

Philip: King Jean has given you some land.

Charles: He has.

Philip: That land belongs to my brother.

Charles: Oooops. Never mind he can have it back, honest.

Philip: He sent me to kill you ... then he can simply take it back.

Charles: (*Wrings his hands pathetically*) I'll be your slave if you spare my life.

Philip: (*Leans forward and looks at Charles nose-to-nose*) No.

Charles: I'll pay you a fortune in gold if you spare my life.

Philip:	No, no.
Charles:	I will go overseas and never return if you spare my life.
Philip:	No. No. No. (*He thrusts his sword in Charles's chest*)
Charles:	Ouch.
Philip:	(*To his men*) Stab him, men.
Soldier:	(*Puzzled cos he's not very bright*) You just stabbed him, boss.
Philip:	Don't argue. Stab him again ... (*they do*) And again ... and again ... and again (*times another 75*)

The killers rush from the room and hurry back to the King of Navarre.

They stabbed Charles d'Espagne EIGHTY times. He died.

The King of Navarre had the nerve to appear before King Jean of France with some of his murdering friends. It was Navarre's turn to grovel and plead for his life. King Jean spared Navarre but had his men arrested and marched off to be hanged.

Suddenly King Jean became tired of the march to the hanging place. He stopped them at a field and ordered their heads lopped off then and there. There was no executioner around, so a soldier was given the job. He wasn't very good. He took six chops to get one head off.

The bodies were hung in chains for two years while Navarre rotted in prison. Navarre mind.

4 Painful Poitiers

One of the 'big' battles of the war was at Poitiers in 1356. The English army was small, but the French made big mistakes – they should have attacked on Sunday when the English were weak, but a bishop told them it was sinful to fight on a Sunday. Then when the French knights did fight it was on foot, not horseback!

CLIP-CLOP
CLIP-CLOP

HOP HOP HOP

The little English army fought desperately for seven hours and finally surrounded the French King Jean II. The French knights fought and died to save him. The French historian Froissart described the battle as very, very bloody…

Some of the French knights are cut in the belly and tread on their own guts. Others vomit their teeth. Some, still standing, have their arms cut off. The dying roll about in the blood of strangers, the fallen bodies groan. The ghosts, flying from the lifeless bodies, moan horribly. The bodies pile up around the waving battle-axe of King Jean. His helmet is knocked off and he bleeds from wounds in the face. 'Surrender,' an English voice cries. 'Surrender or you are a dead man.' A French rebel is the first of the English army to reach the King. 'Give yourself up and I will lead you safely to the English Prince.' King Jean hands him his glove as a sign of surrender.

King Jean II went as a prisoner to England until a vast ransom was paid.

France was left without a king and many parts were 'ruled' by gangs of robbers for almost ten years. (One of the men who tried to take over France was the King's old enemy, the King of Navarre!)

5 Misery Monday

On Monday 13 April 1358 the powerful English army was shattered by an enemy stronger than the French – a storm.

Edward's army was camped near Chartres when a hail-storm hit them. The storm...
- Killed men.
- Killed horses.
- Turned tents to shreds.
- Dragged and crushed the supply wagons into the mud.

Many who survived the storm later died of the cold without any shelter. Shattered King Edward III made peace with the French.

6 Phil the Phighter

King Jean II's son, Philip, was named 'Philip the Bold'. How did he get this wonderful title?

a) Phor phearlessly phighting off phiphty men with just his phists?

b) Phor hitting an unarmed old servant?

Answer: **b)** King Edward of England held a banquet for King Jean of France. The head butler served Edward first. Philip hit the butler and jumped on the table. He cried:

HOW DARE YOU SERVE THE KING OF ENGLAND BEFORE THE KING OF FRANCE?

In other words the King of France was more important than the King of England. But King Edward was a good sport and said:

TRULY COUSIN, YOU ARE PHILIP THE BOLD

The name stuck to Philip like treacle pudding to a spoon. But was Edward being sarcastic? (If you attacked a school dinner lady and jumped on the table would your teacher call you 'bold'?)

7 The G-R-E-A-T invasion flop

William the Conqueror argued with the English – so he invaded. He didn't sit on his bum and wait for the English to come and put the boot into France. So why, in 116 years of war, didn't the French cross the English Channel and invade England?

The answer is: they *tried*.

In 1386 England sent off an army to fight in Spain. The Scots promised to invade England from the north if France crossed the channel to invade from the south. The French began to prepare themselves for the invasion:

- Their fleet was to be 'The greatest since God created the world'. (Well, they bought and built 1,200 ships, but some were a bit ropey.)
- They built a 'camp' that was to be towed across the channel and built into a fortress when they landed. The fortress would be *5.5 kilometres* around the walls. Those walls would be six metres high with towers every 20 metres.
- They had 200,000 arrows (about ten for every English defender) but they'd have been too drunk to fire straight – because they had four *million* litres of wine – enough for 50 litres for each French fighter.

So what went wrong? They waited for the mighty Duke of Berry to arrive but he was too busy collecting things! (He collected books and paintings and musical instruments, the usual stuff. But he also collected dogs and religious 'relics' – bits of holy people and holy things: he had enough of the Virgin Mary's hair to stuff a mattress.)

Berry finally arrived at the port on 14 October – the date when William the Conqueror won the Battle of Hastings – but the days were turning wild and wintry. Storms battered the ships – the sailors lost their bottle.

The King gave up and went home – before he left he gave the floating fortress to the Duke of Burgundy.

The English didn't have four million litres of wine, but they had a pretty good party and a good laugh at the French fighting flops.

8 Awesome Agincourt

After twenty-odd years of peace the English were back. New King Henry V wanted a war so he stirred up the Hundred Years War again.

The small English army met the large French army at Agincourt in 1415. What had the French learned in the 60 years since painful Poitiers?

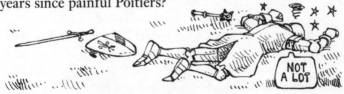

- The French knights fought on foot ... again. Now their armour was heavier to keep out English arrows – but that just meant they could hardly move.
- The French knights pushed to the front to grab the glory. Their crossbows (at the back) were useless. The knights were so packed together they could hardly swing a cat – or a sword.

51

- The French knights slipped in the mud. The next line of knights moved forward and fell over them. The English foot soldiers saw this and dashed in to slide their knives into joints in the armour.

The English were on the rampage again. France had a mad king and a feeble Prince Charles in charge. It was agreed that Henry V and the English could have France when Prince Charles's mad dad died.

It looked like the end for France. But they hadn't reckoned on a simple, village girl...

9 The Mad Maid

Joan of Arc was a French peasant shepherdess. In 1428 she was looking after her sheep in Domremy when she heard heavenly voices. They told her to lead an army against the English.

In just three years she led an army that beat the socks off the English and made sure Prince Charles was crowned King Charles VII.

In the end she was captured by the army of Burgundy and 'sold' to the English. The English didn't like the idea that God was on the French side. They had to prove Joan was actually working for the Devil instead. They put her on trial with French priests to judge her … and, surprise, they found her guilty. She was a witch, they said, so she was burned.

What did King Charles VII of France do to save the girl who had given him his crown and France its freedom?

Nothing. No ransom, no rescue, no bargaining with the English. He let them burn her.

The 1400s were a great time for writing French poetry, but not for Joan. Joan wasn't as famous in her own day as she is in history books now. Maybe someone should have written a song for Joan. If they had it might have gone something like this…

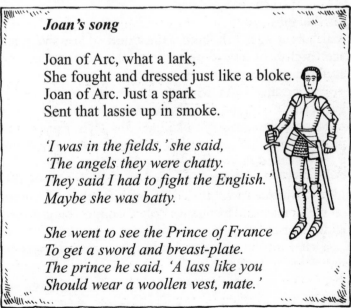

Joan's song

Joan of Arc, what a lark,
She fought and dressed just like a bloke.
Joan of Arc. Just a spark
Sent that lassie up in smoke.

'I was in the fields,' she said,
'The angels they were chatty.
They said I had to fight the English.'
Maybe she was batty.

She went to see the Prince of France
To get a sword and breast-plate.
The prince he said, 'A lass like you
Should wear a woollen vest, mate.'

But Joan she went to Orleans town
And fought and feared for nuffin.
The nasty English all around
They got a fearful stuffin.

At last the English captured her
They tried her with some vicars.
They said, 'You will be sorry when
That fire gets to your knickers.'

Joan of Arc, what a lark,
She fought and dressed just like a bloke.
Joan of Arc. Just a spark
Sent that lassie up in smoke.

10 The end

Joan's fight wasn't the end of the Hundred Years War, but the English never recovered from the defeats they had suffered at her army's hands.

The English had a winning chance against the men of Paris and Aquitaine and Brittany and Normandy, while those regions squabbled like kids. But they had far less chance when the regions joined together under Charles VII and called themselves 'France'.

Suddenly the French people were fighting for a new idea – the idea that they weren't just people of Paris or Aquitaine or Brittany or Normandy ... they were all 'French'.

That's why Joan, even scorched to ashes, was so important in French history.

Cruel crimes

While the Hundred Years War dribbled on there were soldiers everywhere. And, when they weren't fighting, they stayed alive by joining outlaw gangs. They robbed travellers and the French law hadn't the power to stop them. No one was safe on the roads of France – poor pilgrims or travelling traders. There was a saying…

CARRY MONEY AND YOU CARRY DEATH

Crafty Coquillards

In the 1400s the robbers were known as Coquillards. And Coquillards were the only people safe on the roads.

How did you know if a person was a Coquillard?

ACTUALLY YOU CHAPS, I'M ONE OF THOSE COQUILLARD FELLERS MYSELF

PROVE IT

PARIS

The Coquillards had their own way of talking – almost their own language. Have a look at the following and see if you can match the words to their meaning – if you get one wrong you get your throat cut, of course.

COQUILLARD WORD...

1. THE STRAW	2. A HANDLE	3. THE HILL OF JOY	4. A BAFFLE	5. A TAKER
MEANS...				
a. EAR	b. CHEAT	c. PRISON	d. THIEF	e. HANGING TREE

Answers:

1c) Because prison floors were covered in straw. To be 'on the straw' was to be thrown into prison.
2a) Obvious really. Trouble is a Coquillard on the straw could lose his handles as a punishment.
3e) So ending up on the hill of joy is worse than losing your handles.
4b) Hope that answer didn't baffle you.
5d) So obvious you MUST have got this one!

Painful punishments

The only way to put criminals off was to show no mercy to the ones who were caught. Some punishments were nastier than others.

Fried forgers

Only the king was allowed to make money. Forging money was a crime against the king. The punishment? To be boiled in oil.

Now, boiling in oil may not sound too bad – after all most of you do it to potatoes every day then eat them as chips. But in France it was slower and much more painful.

The execution took place in the pig market of Paris. A pot of cool oil was hung over a stone slab. The forger was tied hand and foot and dropped into the oil. A fire was lit under the pot and it took a while for the oil to heat up. The executioner had a long hook to make sure the victim didn't wriggle out. Very slow, very nasty.

Would you want to forge an absence note from your parents if that was the punishment? Taken to the school dinner kitchens where the deep-fat frier awaits you...

← Deep fat friar

Dungeon dread

In 1416 King Charles VI put a big fat tax on the people of Paris. What did they do? Revolted, of course! Nicolas D'Orgemont led a plot to kill the King. What happened? It failed, of course.

Nicolas was a strong man though he was nicknamed Nicolas the Lamer because he lost a foot in an accident when he was young. What punishment could destroy limping Nic?

The underground dungeon of the Bishop of Orleans's palace. He was sent below ground with no light and little air. They said he suffered...

The bread of pain and the water of suffering.

For all his strength Nicolas went mad and died in six months. He was just 46 years old.

Paddled poets

Poetry is quite good for insulting people. You know the sort of thing you write about teachers...

MR BROWN LIKES TO FROWN, HE HAS THE FATTEST FACE IN TOWN

But it wouldn't be a good idea to do it in Middle Ages France. Insulting poets were punished.

The great French poet Francois Villon was found guilty of writing an insulting poem to a lady. His punishment was...

TO BE TIED TO THE BACK OF A CART...

HAVE HIS TROUSERS PULLED DOWN...

BE SPANKED WITH A PADDLE...

BE DRAGGED TO EVERY CROSSROADS IN THE DISTRICT AND HAVE THIS REPEATED

IT'S POETRY IN MOTION

The woman he'd insulted came to watch.

Lucky Villon. Two other poets had insulted a nun and been thrown into jail. But the soldier who wrote a naughty poem about Hugette de Hamel in the 1450s was beaten to death.

Gilles de Rais

Gilles de Rais was the sort of character you usually meet in fairy tales. But if you really want to scare your lousy little brother then don't tell him this story … it's so horrible your little brother would laugh at you and say, 'You're making that up.'

Gilles was a nobleman and a soldier who fought with Joan of Arc. In 1440 he was taken to court and charged with some incredibly horrible crimes. The case was so shocking the judges had a statue of Jesus taken out of the courtroom so the statue didn't have to listen…

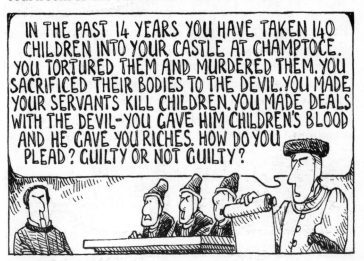

IN THE PAST 14 YEARS YOU HAVE TAKEN 140 CHILDREN INTO YOUR CASTLE AT CHAMPTOCE. YOU TORTURED THEM AND MURDERED THEM. YOU SACRIFICED THEIR BODIES TO THE DEVIL. YOU MADE YOUR SERVANTS KILL CHILDREN. YOU MADE DEALS WITH THE DEVIL-YOU GAVE HIM CHILDREN'S BLOOD AND HE GAVE YOU RICHES. HOW DO YOU PLEAD? GUILTY OR NOT GUILTY?

Gilles de Rais was not amused. He replied…

I REFUSE TO ANSWER. YOU HAVE NO RIGHT TO JUDGE ME. YOU ARE JUST A BUNCH OF CROOKS. YOU'VE BEEN BRIBED TO FIND ME GUILTY. I'D RATHER HANG THAN FACE A COURT FULL OF ROGUES LIKE YOU

This did not make him popular with his judges. The trial went on. They wanted to prove he had used black magic…

Gilles had wasted a lot of money in his life. To get it back he had hired a magician from Italy, Francois Prelati, who said he could change lead into gold. Prelati had wasted a lot more money – and of course failed.

After a month Gilles finally said…

But the court was determined to prove that de Rais had tried to summon the Devil, so they began to call witnesses. It was thought that they'd been paid to lie about Gilles. Prelati, the magician, said…

Then the witnesses to de Rais's kid-killing were called. Gilles de Rais's servant, Etienne Corrilaut, said…

The trial was hardly fair. One accusation was that Gilles killed the son of Jean Lavary, and dumped the boy's body down the castle toilet. But though the evidence was presented in writing, the witnesses who wrote it never actually appeared in court. Gilles's helper, Poitou, confessed, though...

HE WAS DUMPED IN THE TOILET BUT HE FLOATED IN THE TOILET PIT. I HAD TO GO DOWN AND PUSH THE BODY UNDER

Nice job.

The judges asked Gilles again if he was guilty. Gilles admitted the murders but said 'Not guilty' to raising the Devil. This time the judges sent Gilles down to the torture chamber below the court room. They said he should be tortured till he told the truth. So Gilles admitted that the murders had been sacrifices to the Devil. He then made an unusual deal with the court...

YOU HANG ME TILL I'M DEAD-THAT'S FOR THE MURDERS. THEN YOU BURN MY BODY-THAT'S FOR DOING A DEAL WITH THE DEVIL

THAT'S THE SENTENCE

HOW WOULD IT BE IF YOU LET MY FAMILY TAKE MY BODY FROM THE FIRE SO THEY CAN BURY IT?

IT'S A DEAL

So Gilles de Rais was hanged for the murders then his body was burned. The scorched body was taken from the fire – another nice job.

Was he guilty of mass murder? Who knows. He had some very powerful enemies who wanted his lands and castles. When Gilles was executed they got them.

Gilles de Rais may have been the most vicious murderer in French history but he didn't get a very fair trial, so we'll never really know the truth.

Mastering Marelle

The highway robbers of 1400s France didn't spend all their time cutting throats and pinching purses. Oh, no. They enjoyed spending their stolen money as fast as they could in towns like Dijon. There they ate, drank and gambled away their loot. When they lost their money they went out and robbed someone else.

One of their favourite gambling games was called *Marelle*. What was this sport for thugs and ruffians? Rugby? Fencing? Wrestling? No, it was *hopscotch*. Yes, that cute little playground game was a fiercely fought gambling pastime for the highwaymen of Dijon.

Here's how to play it…

You need:
A stone.

A chalk drawn spiral on the ground – like a snail's shell seen from above. The snail is divided into ten squares – they have to be big enough so a player can land in one with each hop.

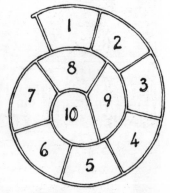

To play:

1 The first player throws the stone at the first square. The stone has to land completely in the square without touching any lines or bouncing out. If not, the player misses that turn. If the player's throw lands in the square, the player hops into the square, picks up the stone and wedges it between their knees. The player hops on to the end of the shape, then turns round and hops back through the shape, hopping through squares in reverse.

2 The players continue in turn by throwing the stone into the next square then the next.

3 A player ends their turn if they step on a line, miss a square or lose their balance. They must start that sequence again on their next turn.

4 The first player who completes one course for every numbered square is the winner.

The prize:

In Marelle you can bet by each player putting money on the last square. If the first player to get to square ten can get back safely with the money they get to keep it.

And you can try to put your opponent off any way you like – so long as you don't touch them.

Teetotum

This is a gambling game with no skill – just luck. Very
popular among the good-for-nothing slubberdegulions of
France. You can try it – gambling for pebbles – just to see
how easy it is to lose a fortune.

You need:
A six-sided pencil. Mark three side of the pencil with the
letters P, J and F. Mark the other three sides with R.

To play:
1 Every player puts one piece of pebble-money into the
middle of the table.
2 Each player takes turns at rolling the pencil.
3 Look at the letter that ends up on top:

R (from the French word 'rien') = you take nothing out,
put nothing in.
P ('piller') = you get your one pebble back – but no more.
J ('jocque') = you put another pebble on to the table.
F ('fors') = you take all the pebbles and have won
the game!

The French gamblers didn't use a pencil – they used a
dice on a spindle that they would spin round. But the idea
was the same. A simple game for simple minds. A group
of teachers would enjoy playing it.

Revolting France

Think of French history and you think of *the* French Revolution – the one that happened in 1789, when lots of posh people got their heads chopped off.

But the French were revolting long before that. In fact, they were expert revolters. Prepare to read about some disgustingly horribly historical happenings…

1 The festering fief of Flanders 1302

Flanders (we call it Belgium now) was a 'fief' of France. (That meant they had to pay taxes to the French.) The fief fellers of Flanders were fed-up though. They had more to do with the English, trading wool and wine with them. So the wild workers of Bruges in Flanders revolted.

The French sent in their foot soldiers and bowmen to soften the fighting fief fellers of Flanders. They were to be followed by the knasty knights to off the pathetic peasants. No contest.

But it all went wrong.

THE FOOT SOLDIERS MARCHED TOWARDS THE MEN OF FLANDERS WHO STOOD ACROSS THE CANALS

FREEDOM FOR FLANDERS

FAH!

BUT THE KNIGHTS WERE IMPATIENT FOR BLOOD. THEY TOLD THEIR FOOT SOLDIERS…

GET BACK AND LET US THROUGH

UH

THE FRENCH KNIGHTS TRAMPLED THE FRENCH FOOT SOLDIERS. THEY HADN'T EVEN REACHED THE FINE FIGHTING FIEF FELLERS OF FLANDERS YET — AND THEY WEREN'T GOING TO. THE KNIGHTS TRIED TO RIDE ACROSS THE CANALS TO GET TO THE ENEMY BUT THE HORSES FLOUNDERED AND THE KNIGHTS FELL. THE FLANDERS FELLERS USED LONG SPIKED AXES (PIKES) TO STAB THE FRENCH LIKE FISH

Fifteen years later the French returned ... it took them a long time to train new knights.

Yes, you could say ... fifteen years after the foul, floundering, falling French foes, and flattened French foot soldiers, had been fixed like fish by the fed-up, fabulous, freedom-fighting fief fellers from Flanders (phew – try saying that with a mouthful of marbles) ... the French massacred the Flanders peasants.

They killed them in their thousands.

2 The pitiful Pastoreaux 1320

The shepherds of France heard that King Louis IX had been thrown in prison. They banded together and said…

The shepherds, or the Pastoreaux as they were known, looked for someone to blame … and started on the priests. They murdered quite a few and then set up their own church with their own Pope and bishops and priests.

Their leader said he had a letter from the Virgin Mary in his fist – but he never opened his hand to show anyone. He said it told the shepherds to fight a Crusade. They marched south towards the Holy Land…

They passed through the towns of Paris and Orleans without much trouble, even though they burned town halls (to stop the tax collectors' work) and broke into prisons.

By the time they reached the south of France they turned their spite against the Jewish people in the region. Jews were accused of getting lepers to poison Christian wells. Five thousand Jews were killed. At Chinon 160 Jews were burned in a pit on an island outside of town. Lepers were blamed for helping the Jews and they were massacred too.

One hundred and twenty Jewish groups were destroyed. At Verdun, 500 Jews defended themselves from inside a stone tower. When they were about to be defeated, they killed themselves.

King Louis (later Saint Louis) thought killing Jews was quite a good idea. But killing his priests wasn't. They had to be stopped.

First French people were ordered not to feed the Pastoreaux. Then the soldiers struck at the Pastoreaux and butchered them.

The Pastoreaux revolt ended with shepherd rebels hanging by their necks from trees.

3 The putrid peasants 1358

The peasants were fed up. They'd lost their king in the Battle of Poitiers against the English – they blamed the knights. And the peasants were being robbed by the bandit-gangs of soldiers – they blamed the knights.

They did what a lot of grumbling people do. They held a meeting. It was on 28 May 1358 in the village of St Leu and they met in a cemetery – the mood was grave.

The answer to the problem of the no-good knights? 'Destroy them all,' the peasants decided and jumped up and down with excited anger – probably trampling over their grandmas' bones as they did so.

They rushed out and murdered the nearest knight and his family then burned his castle.

The idea caught on. Peasants grabbed any old farm tool or weapon and attacked. Many horrors have been described ... but some may not be true. It was said that:

- Some peasants fastened a knight on a meat 'spit' above a fire and roasted him while his wife and children were forced to watch.
- The wife was forced to eat her husband's flesh.
- People who tried to stop them were locked in their houses and the houses set alight.

But when the peasant army came face to face with the crafty King of Navarre, what did he do?

a) Offer to talk to the peasant leader and have him crowned.

b) Offer to talk to the peasant leader and pay him to go home.

I SAY, OLD CHAP, PACK IT IN AND I'LL GIVE YOU MY CROWN OR PERHAPS A BLINKING GREAT BAG OF GOLD

c) Offer to talk to the peasant leader and have him executed.

Answer: **c)** ... and **a)**! Navarre said to the peasant leader, Cade, 'Let's talk at my camp.' The potty peasant agreed. Once Navarre got his hands on Cade he had him crowned – with a red-hot iron crown. That hurt. But not for long because Cade's crowned head was lopped off. What a way to give someone a hair trim. 20,000 rebel peasants ended up dead.

4 Terrible taxes 1379

French lords raised taxes and often used the money to pay for their own fun. In 1379 they charged peasants a tax for a tournament. The people refused to pay. They rioted and the riots spread through France. (Rioting about taxes was going to be good practice for the French Revolution 400 years later.)

Tax collectors went into houses to check what food people had and made them pay tax on it. The people were furious – as you would be if someone marched in to your house, stuck their nose in your fridge and demanded money for your food.

The peasants marched and cried...

Soon the cries turned nastier and became...

They did more than that in southern France, it was said. They did what...?
a) Stole the rich men's food and ate it.
b) Killed the rich men's dogs and ate them.
c) Killed the rich men and ate them.

The revolution ended like most of them when the men in armour marched in. The Duke of Anjou stormed into Montpelier and said…

The next day the Duke said he would let them off most of the savage punishments and the peasants were grateful to him. The threat to massacre 600 was just a little bit of play-acting by the dramatic Duke.

1 Yes, I know, teachers *say* they aren't filthy rich, but those shabby clothes are just a disguise to fool you.

5 The mad Maillotins 1382

The peasants had short memories and were revolting just three years later – and, of course, the nobles gathered an army and crushed them. Nothing new there. But a group of peasant tax-rebels had a few new revolting revolution happenings...

- The rebels started by attacking the Paris police station and stealing 3,000 'Maillotins' – or mallets – for weapons. These lead hammers were pretty deadly if you smashed someone with it. (And very painful if you dropped one on your toe.) The rebels became known as 'Maillotins' even when they weren't carrying a heavy hammer.

- In the south of France 40 of the rebels had a get-rich-quick idea. First you find all the men worth more than a 100 pounds. Next, you kill them. Then, you marry their widows and get their money. There was just one little problem – most of the 40 rebels already had a wife. How did they plan to solve that? They planned to murder their own wives first so they'd be free to marry the rich widows. Nice people.

- The northern rebels were smashed at a battle near Roosebeke. The young King Charles VI asked to see the rebel leader, Artevelde, dead or alive. He was dead.

The young king bravely walked up to Artevelde's corpse and gave it a good kicking. The body was then taken away and hanged from a tree. (Don't worry, it didn't hurt a bit.)

• But the Duke of Burgundy had the strangest little bit of revenge. He had a tapestry woven which showed the face of Artevelde. The Duke then used the tapestry as a carpet so he was able to trample over Artevelde's face when he felt like it.

MAYBE I COULD HAVE HIS FACE PAINTED ON THE BOTTOM OF MY POTTY AS WELL...

6 Revolting students 1453

Paris students were a nuisance. They came from all over Europe and many of them stole food and clothes from the Paris people to stay alive. When house owners tried to argue with the students the students said they didn't understand – they weren't French.

The Paris police finally went potty. They...

• Smashed into student rooms to find stolen goods.

• Arrested students and locked them in jails without food or water.

• Blocked a peaceful student protest march.

• Attacked them with swords, knives, bows and axes as they tried to get past police barriers.

ALLÔ, ALLÔ, ALLÔ

The police had gone too far. Many were punished. Sergeant Jean Charpentier was a killer cop. How was he punished?

a) HE HAD HIS HAND CUT OFF 'LOP!

b) HE HAD HIS NOSE CUT OFF CROP! 'O

c) HE HAD HIS PAY CUT OFF. CAN'T SHOP!

Answer: a) He was dragged through the streets till he reached the house of the man he had murdered. He agreed to pay the widow 400 livres. Then the public executioner lopped off his hand. Which is a bit daft. How could the cruel cop earn the money to pay her when he didn't have a hand?

7 The Protestant protests 1545

By the middle of the 1500s England had become a Protestant country. France was still Catholic and worried that the Protestant ideas might spread over there.

So what do *you* do to a Protestant?

WE TAKE HIM TO SCHOOL AND TEACH HIM HOW GOOD IT IS TO BE CATHOLIC!

WE LET HIM GET ON WITH IT. HE'S DOING US NO HARM

WE EXECUTE HIM AND HIS FRIENDS. THAT'LL PUT A STOP TO THEM

Which do you think they did in France in 1545? Here's an extra clue…

AS WELL AS BEING A PROTESTANT HE HAS SOME LAND I WANT

Got it? That's right, the Protestants were executed. In Provence Baron Jean Meynier wanted some land from a Protestant neighbour. He went to King Francis I with a rumour that the Protestants were planning a rebellion.

Protestant women were shut in a church and it was set on fire. Protestant men were sent to serve as slaves rowing galleys for the French navy. Protestant homes were forced open and robbed.

Did mean, malevolent Meynier get the land he wanted? Of course he did.

Some rebellions weren't rebellions at all. They were set up as an excuse to exterminate someone...

8 The Bartholomew batterings 1572
The peasants usually revolted because they had no food. But in the 1560s the Protestants had a much more dangerous idea...

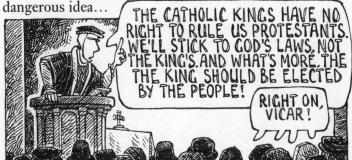

Don't obey the king? Elect a new one? That was revolution. The Catholics were shocked.

Food prices were high in the 1560s (again) and hungry Catholic peasants looked for someone to blame. Guess who?

The St Bartholomew's Day Massacre in 1572 was a good excuse to do just that.

On August 22, the Protestant leader, Admiral de Coligny, was riding through Paris when an assassin fired at him, breaking his arm.

The Catholic assassins decided to finish him off and went to King Charles IX to see if he agreed. Charles argued…

76

The butchering began…

- That night a troop of soldiers went to de Coligny's door. They killed the guard who opened the door, and rushed into the house. De Coligny was dragged from his bed and stabbed in the belly till his guts spilled out.

- De Coligny, still alive, was then thrown out of his bedroom window to the pavement below. The Catholic Duke de Guise kicked the corpse in the face and claimed, 'This is what the King ordered.'

- Everyone thought, 'Oh, *that's* what the King wants?' So the rest of the Catholics in Paris joined in. Catholics wore white crosses on their hats, and went around butchering their Protestant neighbours with the help of soldiers.

- The killing went on for three days or so, with the King unable to bring the whole thing under control.

- The massacres spread outside of Paris over the next few months. Some thought they had orders from the Crown to kill all the Protestants.

- Many people gave up their Protestant religion. Yet again a rebellion had been crushed by cruelty.

77

Wedding woe

A wedding is usually a happy event. Loads of booze and dancing and laughter … and murder if you were at the wedding of Henry of Navarre.

Henry was a hated Protestant. Thousands of his Protestant supporters arrived in Paris for his wedding to Margaret, the King's sister. Unfortunately the Catholics turned up as well – invited by the King – and the wedding became a bloodbath. In this massacre:

- In Paris 2,700 Protestants died that day and around France another 20,000 were killed around that time.
- Margaret saved some Protestants by hiding them under her bed.
- Young women insisted on seeing the corpses to see if they could find their missing boyfriends.

Henry of Navarre knew he could only survive the massacre if he pretended to turn Catholic. And Henry knew he could become king and rule Paris if he went to a Catholic church for a service the Catholics call 'mass'. So Henry did it and 17 years after the massacre he finally took the throne. He said, famously…

Paris is worth a mass.

Henry became Henry IV – so he got all France for the price of a few Catholic prayers. He brought peace and became known as Good King Henry – which isn't bad.

9 Cruelty to Croquants 1592

Stop me if you've heard this one but … the peasants were starving because of poor harvests and the lords were still taxing them.

What did the peasants do? Revolt.

What did the lords do? Kill them cruelly.

Same old story. The difference this time was King Henry IV said…

> *Can't say I blame them. If I was a peasant I'd revolt.*

But these Croquant revolts went on for nearly 50 years. Always the same. Peasants revolt – peasants massacred. They just didn't learn.

In 1637 the Duke de la Valette attacked and killed 1,000–1,500 Croquants. The Duke's men then burnt 25 houses with women and children still inside.

Survivors suffered the usual: torture, breaking on the wheel (more details later), hanging, chopping off body-bits and showing those bits in public. Some were sentenced to life as a slave in the galley ships.

79

Did you know…?

The peasants expected the executioners to do a good, clean job. If an executioner made a mess of an execution then the spectators could turn on him and lynch him too.

Sometimes the victims were heroes to the peasants so they helped them escape. They would…

- Have a riot at the scaffold and set the prisoner free in the confusion.
- Cut through the wooden steps up to the scaffold so the executioner had an accident.

- Simply rush onto the scaffold and kidnap the prisoner.

10 Cracking Camisards 1702

The Croquants were battered – but they had started fighting back against the executioners. In 1702 the Camisards revolted, fighting for their religion – nothing new there – but King Louis XIV's punishments were so harsh the rebels rebelled against them. The rebellion went on much longer – three years – than it could have done.

One of cruel Louis XIV's punishments was 'breaking on the wheel.' So, if your teachers have a problem with a rebel pupil, here's a handy Louis XIV guide to dealing with them. You may like to pass it on to your teacher…

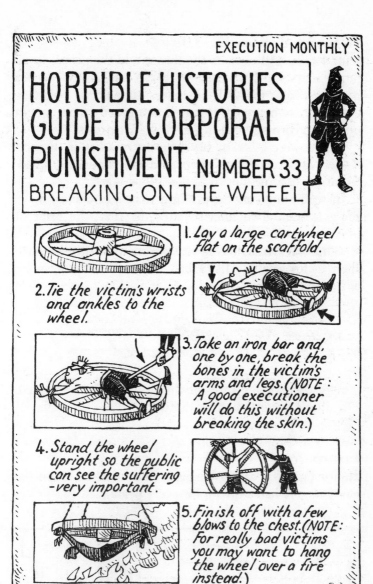

EXECUTION MONTHLY

HORRIBLE HISTORIES GUIDE TO CORPORAL PUNISHMENT NUMBER 33
BREAKING ON THE WHEEL

1. Lay a large cartwheel flat on the scaffold.

2. Tie the victim's wrists and ankles to the wheel.

3. Take an iron bar and, one by one, break the bones in the victim's arms and legs. (NOTE: A good executioner will do this without breaking the skin.)

4. Stand the wheel upright so the public can see the suffering – very important.

5. Finish off with a few blows to the chest. (NOTE: For really bad victims you may want to hang the wheel over a fire instead.)

This was still happening about 30 times a year in the 1780s in France. It's no wonder the people were so violent when they revolted in 1789.

11 The Flour Wars 1775

King Louis XVI came to the throne and the people loved him ... at first. The price of bread had always been a problem. So Louis XVI's ministers came up with plans to cut the price of bread. But rich and greedy men bought up all the corn and charged even higher prices.

There were riots in nearly every market in France. Rioters attacked bakers' shops and stole flour and bread. The riots became known as the 'Flour Wars'.

Instead of making the peasants happy, Louis had made them furious. Two months after the riots the price of bread was still high.

What did Louis do? Had his coronation with the usual show of his wealth. His Queen, Marie Antoinette, wrote to her mother...

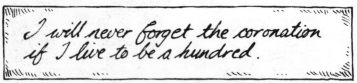

I will never forget the coronation if I live to be a hundred.

The peasants made sure she didn't live to be a hundred. She didn't forget – neither did they.

Funny food

Henry IV was a caring king. He said he cared about the peasants. He had a dream for every peasant in France...

I want to see every peasant have a chicken in the pot.

HOORAY HENRY!

MUMMY – WHAT'S A CHICKEN?

The chickens, who didn't speak French, might have been the only ones to disagree.

Henry's dream didn't really come true, of course. Most peasants stayed hungry:

- Peasants only ate meat a few times a year – on feast days or when they slaughtered their animals in the winter.
- They didn't even get the kilo of bread a day that they needed to stay healthy.
- About a quarter of children died before their first birthday and half of all the children born in France were dead before their tenth birthday.

French peasants never seemed to have enough food while their kings and queens had too much. So food became one of the biggest reasons for revolt.

The French are famous for their cooking. Delicious snails and frogs' legs are still favourite foods of France. All of which has nothing to do with this joke...

Scoffing stories

French peasants were so interested in food half their folk stories were about it. Like the story of the greedy peasant girl...

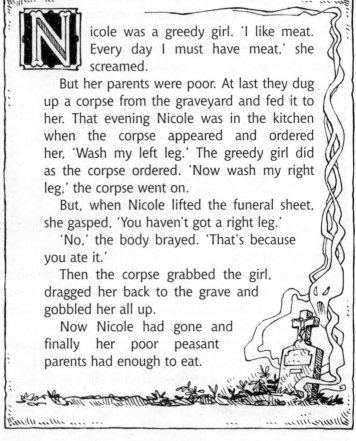

icole was a greedy girl. 'I like meat. Every day I must have meat,' she screamed.

But her parents were poor. At last they dug up a corpse from the graveyard and fed it to her. That evening Nicole was in the kitchen when the corpse appeared and ordered her, 'Wash my left leg.' The greedy girl did as the corpse ordered. 'Now wash my right leg,' the corpse went on.

But, when Nicole lifted the funeral sheet, she gasped, 'You haven't got a right leg.'

'No,' the body brayed. 'That's because you ate it.'

Then the corpse grabbed the girl, dragged her back to the grave and gobbled her all up.

Now Nicole had gone and finally her poor peasant parents had enough to eat.

That's just a story. But here are a few fantastic French food facts to flabbergast you...

1 Bad booze

In the Middle Ages the richest wine was the deep red wine from Gascony. Wine sellers often took cheap red wine, added dye to it and sold it as expensive Gascony wine. You wouldn't know till you drank it – and discovered it stained your teeth and tongue dark red.

2 Beastly buns

In 1590 Paris was under siege and the people were starving. They went along to the Cemetery of the Innocents and pinched the bones. They ground them up, mixed them with water, and baked them into bread.

3 Lousy loaves

In 1586 there was a famine in the Vivarais region of France. The people had a few handfuls of barley or oats for flour. They made their bread more filling by grinding in tasty extra 'flour' made from...

- Acorns
- Grape seeds
- Pine tree bark
- Nut shells
- Broken tiles and bricks.

That's tough but tasteless. But imagine eating the bread they made from grass and sheep guts.

4 Munching monarchs

Louis XIV was famous for his mountainous meals. But Louis XVI wasn't much better. At one wedding party young Louis stuffed himself so full he couldn't move.

5 Greedy guts

While Louis XVI was feasting a dreadful plague and famine swept through northern France. Tanners took cattle and turned their skins into leather. The meat was sold to the butchers but the guts were thrown into the back streets. The starving people fought over the cow guts, kidneys, liver and brains because they had nothing else to eat.

Some mothers who couldn't feed babies left them out in the wind and rain to die.

Peasants were found dead in ditches, their mouths full of grass that they'd tried to eat.

And King Louis grew fatter.

6 Sliced bread

Most people think sliced bread was invented in the twentieth century. But when the French Revolution locked Louis XVI in prison in 1792 he was fed on sliced bread.

Stretch your brain cell and work out why? Why didn't the guards give him the usual loaf of bread?

Answer: They were worried that the King's friends might smuggle messages into the prison and help him escape. It would be easy to write a message, bake it into a loaf and send it to the King. So the guards sliced the bread first.

Kurious kings

The kings of France had more money than they could spend while their people starved. No wonder there were revolts. And apart from the wasters, some kings were just plain potty.

France, like most other countries in history, has had some pretty peculiar people in charge. And their names were even odder. Spot the only invented name in this motley crew:

Answer: Pepin the Potato was NOT a king of France. The rest were.

Here is some incredible info and foul facts about a few of France's rulers.

Louis I (788–840)
Known as Louis the Pious (or 'Saintly'). This kind and holy king discovered Bernard of Italy was plotting against him. So he kindly had Bernard's eyes gouged out.

Sadly this killed Bernard. Saintly Louis was said to be very upset. What a kind man.

Philip IV the Fair (1268–1314)

Philip did a bad job of running the country and the peasants were starving and after his blood. He came up with a vicious way to raise money – and save his skin.

- Philip accused a group of fighting monks – called 'Knights Templar' – of worshipping the Devil.
- Philip had them tortured and then burned at the stake.
- Philip was able to steal the Templars' money and buy his way out of trouble.

But it did Philip the very-unfair no good because the Templars had a spooky revenge...

The chief Templar (the Grand Master), was sent to the stake to be burned. Pope Clement had agreed to the execution. As the flames leapt up the Grand Master cried to Philip, 'I shall meet you and Clement by God's seat before a year is past. You and your family, for 13 generations, will be cursed!' Pope Clement died the next month ... King Philip died within seven months, though he was a healthy 46-year-old.

Charles VI (1368–1422)

The trouble with having kings and queens is this: what do you do if one of them goes a little potty? You can't sack a monarch, can you?

Charles VI of France became mad and all France suffered. Here's his sad story…

1 In 1385 he married Isabeau – but only after he had her examined in the nude. She was the daughter of Stephen III, Duke of Upper Bavaria-Ingolstadt – known as Stephen the Toff.

2 Charles fell ill – his hair fell out and his nails fell off. Before he recovered he got a terrible shock. In 1392 Charlie's friend, Olivier de Clisson, was attacked – but survived more than '60 blows by sword and knife'. The King flipped.

3 Charles set out with an army to get de Clisson's attacker. On the journey he started babbling nonsense and making rude signs with his hands.

4 One hot day Charles rode out after drinking too much wine. A leper jumped out, grabbed the reins of Charles's horse and cried, 'Turn back, your Highness. You are destroyed.' This scare tipped the King over the edge into complete madness.

5 A little further on that journey a page dropped the King's lance with a clatter. The frightened Charles drew his sword and chopped at everyone in sight. He killed five of his own knights before his attendants stopped him.

6 Charles recovered but, a year later, suffered another night of terror. Charles went to a fancy dress party dressed as a wild man. His friends

were dressed the same. Their costumes were covered in tar. A spark from a flaming torch set them alight. Four died and Charles was only saved by a duchess who threw her skirt over him.

7 Charles began to imagine he was made of glass. He had steel rods put into his clothes so he wouldn't shatter if he fell over.

8 Charles started to insist his name was George. He refused to change his clothes for months. He stank and his body was crawling with lice. The doctor decided he needed a shock. Ten men with blackened faces rushed into his bedroom. Terrified Charles changed his clothes. (Wouldn't you?)

9 Charles suspected everyone – especially his wife, Queen Isabeau. Her trusted servant, Louis de Bosredon, was thrown in prison in chains. Which was better than what happened next. He was put in a leather sack and drowned in the River Seine. Louis was in Seine – Charles was simply insane.

10 They treated Charles with around 250 oranges – and it cured him for a little while. A year later he died of a fever. During the reign of poor Charles the French knights had lost the Battle of Agincourt to a little English army. It was time for a new king – and an even crazier woman, Joan of Arc – to save France.

Charles VIII (1470–1498)

Charlie was so polite he didn't turn his head away from his wife while he talked to her and led her into his tennis court. As a result he smacked his head against a beam, cracked his skull and died. Game, set and match, Charlie.

Francis I (1494–1547)

Rich Francis got Leonardo da Vinci to paint him a picture. It became the most famous picture in the world – the *Mona Lisa*. Where did filthy-rich Francis hang this painting? In his bathroom.

Francis restarted the wars with Italy – and he came unstuck at the battle of Pavia…

Francis believed that knights were gentlemen and should fight like gentlemen – on horses, with swords and lances. His army had guns but he wouldn't let them fire.

Francis and his knights charged at the Italian guns, waving their swords. Of course the Italians shot them down. Francis's horse was shot from under him and he was captured.

Six thousand French soldiers died – all because Francis wanted to fight like a gentleman.

Henry VIII of England had been a rival of Francis all their lives. So Francis laughed when he heard that Henry was dead. Then he remembered that Henry had said, 'One day we'll both be dead.' Francis was upset, and the same night had a fever. He never recovered. You can just imagine Henry's ghost…

Henry II (1519–1559)

Henry's dad, Francis I, should have told the lad: 'Knights in armour are finished.' Maybe they did tell Henry – maybe he just didn't listen. He played at being a knight by fighting in a tournament. So you can't feel sorry when he had a bit of an accident…

⚜

10 July 1559

News from the French Court

It is with deep sadness that we announce the death of King Henry. Ten days ago he took part in a tournament to celebrate his daughter's marriage. He beat several knights but said he wanted one last charge, even though he was tired. He asked Gabriel de Montgomery to fight him.

De Montgomery begged the King not to fight. King Henry insisted.

> *The two men put on their helmets, mounted their horses and charged at one another with their lances. De Montgomery's lance shattered and splinters went into Henry's face. After ten days in agony the King has died.*
> *His sickly 15-year-old son, Francis II, has become the new King of France.* ⚜

ARRANGE THE FOLLOWING WORDS INTO A WELL-KNOWN PHRASE OR SAYING: HIM-RIGHT-SERVES

DRIP DRIP

Charles IX (1550–1574)

Charles allowed his Catholic friends to massacre their Protestant enemies on St Bartholomew's Day in 1572 ... then spent the next two years feeling really, really sorry for what had happened.

Then, in 1574 he stopped feeling sorry. He died. It was said he was tormented with guilt for the massacres and died sweating blood. (This is a horrible way to die and it makes a right mess of the bedclothes so try not to do it. Think of the poor person who has to clean up after you.)

Henry III (1551–1589)

People who live by the sword often die by the sword, it is said. Henry III was a great example. Horrible Henry fought against the Guise family and viciously killed the Duke of Guise in December 1588.

First he invited the Duke of Guise to meet him. There were rows of Henry's archers lining the stairs but the daft Duke went on up them. There were 40 armed men in the King's room ... but the daft Duke went in. Would you have been a bit suspicious by now?

When he went in, the doors were bolted. The Duke struggled bravely, but he didn't stand a chance against horrible Henry...

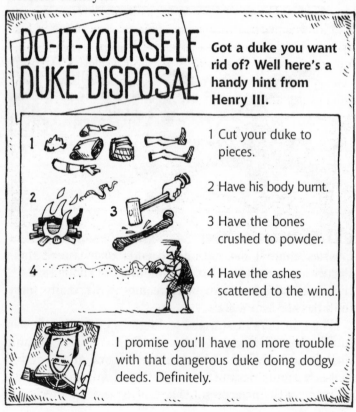

DO-IT-YOURSELF DUKE DISPOSAL

Got a duke you want rid of? Well here's a handy hint from Henry III.

1 Cut your duke to pieces.

2 Have his body burnt.

3 Have the bones crushed to powder.

4 Have the ashes scattered to the wind.

I promise you'll have no more trouble with that dangerous duke doing dodgy deeds. Definitely.

Henry then did the same to the Duke's brother, the Cardinal de Guise.

BUT … horrible Henry didn't last long. In August 1589 he was dead. Murdered.

A monk called Jacques Clement asked to see the King and the guards let him in. As soon as he was close enough he drew a knife and stabbed Henry to death.

The Duke of Guise's ghost must have laughed its ghostly socks off. What happened to the mad monk? The King's servants battered and hacked him to death.

You wouldn't believe how the next king, Henry IV, died…

Henry IV (1553–1610)

King Henry IV was killed by a mad monk. (I said you wouldn't believe it. But it's true.) Henry was riding in his carriage when it got stuck in a traffic jam. Mad Monk, Francois Ravaillac, jumped on to the carriage wheel and thrust his dagger into the King's chest. The King then said a pretty silly thing.

I've been stabbed!

Amazing man. He is dying, and he still finds the time to tell his doctors exactly what his problem is. How thoughtful.

The blood gushed from his mouth. The doctors couldn't help him. He died.

Louis XIII (1601–1643)

Little Louis was just eight when he became king. So, of course, his mum ran the country for him. The trouble was his mum had a boyfriend, Concino Concini, who helped her to run the country. When Louis XIII was 15 the young lad gave the order...

- Guards went to arrest Concino Concini. They said he had struggled so they had to shoot him three times in the head and stab him before kicking the body aside. In fact Concino Concini was murdered. That's what Louis really wanted.
- The body was buried secretly – but not secretly enough. A mob of Paris people dug up the hated Concino Concini, chopped the body into bits, fed some to their dogs and burned the rest.
- Concini's wife was then put on trial and beheaded. She was a rich woman. Who got her money? Louis XIII, of course.

Two years later in 1619, Mum tried to lead a rebellion against her own son. She failed. Happy families or what?

Louis XIV (1638–1715)

The French don't have kings these days. But they still look back at some of them and say (in French) 'He was a good guy ... for a king.' And one of their favourites is Louis XIV – nicknamed 'The Sun King'.

His vast palace at Versailles cost millions in today's money and it had over a thousand fountains in its gardens.

Just one cloak in his wardrobe cost Louis a sixth of the cost of the palace – while his peasants starved.

Here are a few facts about the French favourite…

1 Louis was a bit of a piggy eater. When he died it was discovered that his bowels were twice as long as most people's and his stomach was huge. But was he a greedy eater because he had a big gut to fill? Or did he have a big gut because he ate so much?

2 Louis built the palace of Versailles and you can still visit it today. The palace had golden ceilings and 5,000 servants – but only two toilets. Rich visitors had to take their own potties with them. They were emptied in a ditch at one corner of the palace – and Louis made sure unpopular guests had their rooms just above that dreadful ditch.

3 Louis was a big-head – and a bald head. No one but his hairdresser was allowed to see the King without his wig. Louis set a fashion in Europe for wigs. These wigs were usually made from goats' hair – very itchy – and were probably full of lice and other insects. He was also a bit of a shorty and wore high-heeled shoes. They were the height of fashion.

4 Louis was very fussy about good manners in his palace. He even invented some new manners:

- No one was allowed to turn their back on the royal family – or even a picture of the royals.
- No one was allowed to go to the toilet while travelling with the king – a duchess travelled with Louis in a coach and was desperate for a pee but she had to wait nearly six hours.
- Knocking on the door was said to be rude so palace people had to scratch on them with their fingernails. Screech.

5 Louis wanted total power – power with no limit. One of his lords, the Count de Guiche, argued with the King...

The Count did something no one dared do – he turned his back on the King and marched to the door...

6 Louis liked to sleep in his own bed – wherever he was. So he had 413 beds made and there was always one handy wherever he stopped for the night. But he wasn't so fussy about his baths. How many baths did he have in his whole life?

a) 77 (one a year)

b) 924 (one a month)

c) 3

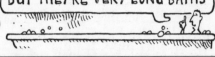

Answer: c) Phew! So it's not that surprising that he didn't notice how mouldy he was. One day he pulled off a sock and one of his toes dropped off.

7 When Louis XIV's queen died he married the Marquise de Maintenon. He kept the marriage a secret. His new wife was fondly known as 'Old Prune Face' and 'The Rag-Bag'.

8 Louis died in 1715 saying, 'Sorry I spent so much money and went into so many wars with other countries.' He was. His son and grandson were dead and Louis XIV decided this was God's punishment because he'd been such a lousy Louis. Louis's five-year-old great-grandson took the throne. Guess what he was called? That's right…

Louis XV (1710–1774)

What a lazy Louis he turned out to be. He let ministers like Cardinal Fleury run the country. When Fleury died Louis decided to take over. Who told him how to rule? His girlfriends, Madame de Pompadour and Madame du Barry.

No wonder Robert Damiens (known as 'Robert the Devil.') tried to assassinate him. In 1757 Robert the Devil was caught and sentenced to death.

The mob may have felt a bit sorry for King Louis ... but the punishment of Robert was so vicious they felt sorry for Robert the Devil instead.

Big mistake, Louis.

Louis XVI (1754–1793)

Another Louis – the grandson of the last one. This was the king who finally got the chop. What was so wrong with lousy little Louis XVI?

Louis never really wanted to be king. He was shy, clumsy … and silly as a big daft kid!

Why not try these jolly games at school? See how much detention you can get for each one!

101

But France wasn't happy with its silly king. Between 1788 and 1793 there were nearly 5,000 acts of rebellion in France ... and then Louis lost his head on the guillotine.

Louis everywhere

England stopped having Henries when they got to Henry VIII and Edwards when they got to Edward VIII. But France loved the name Louis and they kept going past eight – the Louis who lost his head in the Revolution was number 16 ... and when they brought kings back for a while in the early 1800s they went up to Louis XVIII. What was the matter with these people? Couldn't they think of a new name? Or were they just too lazy? Anyway, the days of the new Louis kings were just as horrible as the old ones.

Quirky queens and wicked women

France had some crazy kings and some cruel kings in its history. But those miserable monarchs also had some weird and wacky women to share their thrones and their lives ... quirky queens and wicked women.

Jeanne of Burgundy (1294–1322)

Philip V's wife was a wicked lady. Before Philip became king she was spied having a bit of a party with two sisters-in-law and three fellers. The fellers were murdered and one of her sisters-in-law was suffocated between two mattresses.

But Philip forgave Jeanne and the happy couple went on to become king and queen.

Philip died and Jeanne moved to the Tower of Nesle – the tower where she'd been spied on – and went on with her naughty ways. For another seven years it was said that Jeanne...

- Spotted men walking past and invited them up to her tower.
- After a kiss and a cuddle she tied them up in a sack and had them lowered to drown in the river below.

The tower was known as the Screaming Tower and was finally knocked down in 1665.

Marie de Medici (1573–1643)

This French queen wore the dearest dress in the history of the world. It had 3,000 diamonds and 39,000 pearls on it. The dress would cost you ten million pounds today.

She wore it just once. And the peasants starved.

Marie Louise of Orléans (1695–1719)

Marie Louise has been seen as a fat figure of fun. In fact she probably suffered an eating disorder, bulimia. Her tragic story is not a pretty one…

The Duke of Saint-Simon said:

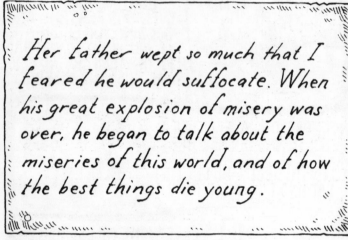

Her father wept so much that I feared he would suffocate. When his great explosion of misery was over, he began to talk about the miseries of this world, and of how the best things die young.

Marie Louise's dad died four years later.

Marie Antoinette (1755–1793)

A fortune-teller read Marie Antoinette's horoscope when she was born. He said her life would be a disaster. A birth party for the baby Marie was cancelled. That fortune-teller knew what he was talking about.

Marie Antoinette grew up and married Louis XVI. Bad move. She was Austrian, yet she became the most famous victim of the French Revolution when her head hit the basket.

The peasants hated her. She stood for everything bad about the nobles who ruled France. Was she as bad as all that? Test your teacher with this quick quiz. Of course, if they score less than seven out of six, they lose their heads...

True or false...?

1 Marie Antoinette was born Maria Antonia. (That's true.) She had six sisters: Maria, Maria, Maria, Maria, Maria ... and Maria.

2 A young man asked Marie to marry him when they were both very young. (That's true.) He grew up to be the famous composer Mozart.

3 When Marie Antoinette arrived in France for her wedding she had to take all her clothes off and be examined to see if she was good enough for husband Louis.

4 Marie arrived in France in 1770 and it took the French 23 years to hack her head off. (That's true.) But the people of Paris hated her from the start.

5 Marie had a friend, Madame de Guéméne, who always had her dogs with her. (That's true.) Madame de Guéméne's dogs helped her to speak to spirits of dead people.

6 When the Revolution came Marie Antoinette worried that someone might break into her room and try to kill her. (That's true.) As a burglar alarm she kept a budgie by her bedside.

Answers:

1 True. All the girls in her family were christened with the first name Maria. Their mother was Maria Theresa. Very confusing except when it came to dinner time and their nurse called, 'Dinner, Maria.' When Maria Antonia moved to France to be Queen the French changed her names to the French 'Marie' and 'Antoinette'.

2 True. At least that's the story Mozart's dad told. Little Wolfgang Mozart slipped on his musical backside at a court concert. Little Marie Antoinette rushed over, helped him to his little musical feet and kissed him. The boy said, 'I am so grateful I will marry you, if you want.' It may have been better for her neck if she'd accepted. Then she married her brother! Louis XVI didn't come from France for the wedding – Marie Antoinette's brother took the bridegroom's place and instead of saying 'I do,' said 'Louis does.'

3 False ... but that's what several historians have written. Don't believe everything you read.

4 False. When Marie Antoinette went into Paris she was mobbed by adoring French people. They broke through police barriers and Marie and hubby Louis couldn't move for three-quarters of an hour. It took a very special sort of woman to turn all that love into murdering hate.

5 True. At least that's what she said. What were they? Spectre spaniels? Ghostie greyhounds? Poltergeist pugs?

6 False. She kept a little dog under her bed. Of course people in those days also kept a potty under the bed in case they needed a pee in the middle of the night. Let's hope Marie didn't get the potty mixed up with the dog's water-bowl in the dark!

Madame Roland

Madame Roland hated Marie Antoinette, and was one of the few women with influence after the 1789 revolution, through her husband a minister of the new Republic. She said…

Peace is no good. We can only go forward with blood.

Charming. She wrote…

My skin is of a dazzling colour. My mouth may be a little large but it has the sweetest smile. My hands are small and perfect showing my cleverness and grace. My teeth are white and perfect. These are my treasures.

In 1793 her perfect white teeth bit the basket when she went to the guillotine. Wonder if she was wearing her sweetest smile?

Did you know…?

In 1774 Miss Bertin of Paris had a fashion shop and she came up with a new idea for women's heads … 'poufs'. These were stiff net things built on top of the head and then decorated. Some were decorated with flowers.

But there were also some other very strange sights that posh Paris women carried on their heads. Can you spot the odd one out?

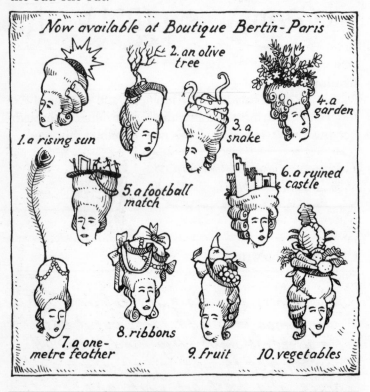

Now available at Boutique Bertin-Paris

1. a rising sun
2. an olive tree
3. a snake
4. a garden
5. a football match
6. a ruined castle
7. a one-metre feather
8. ribbons
9. fruit
10. vegetables

Answer: 5 is the odd one out. There is no record of Miss Bertin making a football scene in a pouf. But all the rest are true. Queen Marie Antoinette had 1, 2 and 3 all together on her head at the same time.

Savage seventeenth century

This was the age when the kings of France were really rich and started to see themselves as perfect – if the king said jump you didn't argue, you just asked, 'How high?'

Some things didn't change. Wars? Rebellions? That's right...

1618 Remember the Hundred Years War? Now the Thirty Years War starts in Germany. France will join in later. They don't believe in short sharp scraps these French, do they?
1630s Now the French decide to fight Austria. This will cost lots of money to pay their armies. So Ministers Cardinal Richelieu and Mazarin tax the peasants. Taxes treble by 1648 – and the peasants have riots and rebellions. (Surprised?)
1661 Louis XIV (the Sun King) takes the throne – he's there to stay a l-o-n-g time. He will build the glorious (but expensive) palace of Versailles. He will also go to war against the Brits (again) and try to grab new lands for France around the world. He wants a French Empire.
1690 Terrible famines in Northern France. Starving peasants, as usual.

Rotten Richelieu (1585–1642)

During the 1600s, the idea of France as a single country under a single king became really strong. One man ruthlessly plotted to make sure it became a reality. That man was Cardinal Armand Jean du Plessis de Richelieu.

Richelieu was a top Catholic bishop – a 'cardinal' – but that didn't stop him becoming a top minister to Louis XIII (the lovely Louis who had his mum's boyfriend murdered).

Richelieu was as ruthless as Louis. They made a good pair. The Cardinal had this idea that a king should have total power over his people. Louis liked that – but no one asked the people what they thought of the idea.

Richelieu also thought it was a good idea to go to war with most of the rest of Europe. That was an expensive business so he raised taxes that the peasants had to pay. They revolted. They hated the 'Salt Tax' and in 1639 they had…

The Barefoot rebellion

The 'Barefoot' rebellion started in the salt marshes of Avranches where people worked in bare feet making salt at the edge of the sea (it wasn't that they couldn't afford shoes). Many of the people who joined the rebels were priests, army officers and even a few nobles. For once the farming peasants didn't give the rebs much support.

So what do you do when a tax collector calls? Easy. In 1639 the 'Barefoot' rebels had the answer…

FIRST LIE YOUR TAX COLLECTOR DOWN ON THE ROAD

TAKE YOUR HEAVIEST CART AND ROLL IT OVER HIM

That must be one of the oddest rebellion cries of all time.

The King left Cardinal Richelieu to sort out the peasants. End of rebellion.

Did you know…?
Richelieu probably had lessons in ruthlessness from his deadly dad…

It all started when Uncle Richelieu was murdered by a neighbour in 1565. Daddy Richelieu set out for revenge. As the murderer crossed a stream Daddy Richelieu rolled a huge cartwheel at him and knocked him off his horse. Before he could get up Daddy Richelieu had butchered him in the stream.

Twenty years later Cardinal Richelieu was born. You can imagine what he learnt at Daddy's knee…

113

Musketeer Mystery

Richelieu's days were made famous in the book 'The Three Musketeers'. Musketeers were soldiers armed with musket guns but also pretty handy with their swords. Richelieu used them to do his dirty work.

Brief pause for an ancient historical joke…

When France was being invaded by Spain in 1641, the leader of the invaders, Soissons, was hunted down and shot by one of Richelieu's musketeers … it is said.

But there is another story about the death of Soissons. Soissons wore a helmet with a face guard. It was his habit to push up the face guard with his pistol. In his last battle he pushed up the guard with a loaded pistol – the pistol went off and blew his head open.

Pointless plot

On 12 September 1642 the Marquis of Cinq-Mars was beheaded. His crime? He had plotted with his friend, de Thou, to assassinate Cardinal Richelieu.

The execution was very entertaining. A witness may have described it like this…

114

Dear Mum

Saw the execution of the plotters Cinq-Mars and De Thou today. What a laugh! The man De Thou was very quiet and a bit shaky. But Cinq-Mars strutted around like he was the star of the show — well, I suppose he was!

First Cinq-Mars says to the executioner, 'I say my good man. I am much more important than De Thou. My execution block should be on a higher platform than his.'

'What?' the executioner says. 'You want me to start building a new platform? Now?'

'That's right,' Cinq-Mars says.

'Stuff that,' the executioner says, 'just get your hat off and kneel down.'

The crowd were enjoying this. We didn't half laugh when Cinq-Mars says, 'No. I won't take my hat off. I only take my hat off for the King or for God. Not for a common axeman like you.'

The crowd cheered and you could see the executioner shaking. Well, I mean, it wasn't supposed to happen like that. Anyway Cinq-Mars finally agrees to take his hat off and he throws it into the crowd. You should have seen the scrabbling and punching that went on to get a bit of that hat.

At last Cinq-Mars lays his head on the block and the crowd cheer for him. The executioner raises the axe and you can see it shaking. Chop! He brings the axe down and misses. The bloke next to me says, 'Proper executioner has a broken arm. This is just an assistant'.

Well, Mum, I won't go into the gory details, but it took the lad a lot of chops to get that head off and the crowd were pretty angry. When the head finally comes off they charge up onto the platform and batter the executioner with his own axe. I think they killed him.

Anyway, it was all very entertaining. You should have been here Mum, you missed a real good laugh.

Your loving son, Raoul xxx

When Cinq-Mars had been executed Richelieu wrote to the King and said he wanted even more power. The King said, 'Yes.'

Richelieu was happy. Dead happy. A fortnight later Richelieu was simply dead. (Just a chest infection, not murder.)

What a shame for Cinq-Mars though. He plotted to kill Richelieu and was executed – if he'd waited just three months the Cardinal would have been dead anyway.

People lit bonfires to celebrate the death of the cruel and crafty Cardinal. And, another six months later, King Louis XIII had died too.

Pointy poet

One of Richelieu's strongest beliefs was that duelling was wrong – as it was murder – and had to be banned.

Between 1601 and 1609 there were 2,000 French noblemen killed in duels.

One of the fittest and fastest fighters was the poet, Cyrano de Bergerac.

Cyrano had a big nose – a huge nose – a nose that would have looked right on Pinocchio. If anyone poked fun at the nose (or Pinocched fun at it) then Cyrano challenged them to a sword fight.

He won over 1,000 duels. At his peak he was slicing, slashing and stabbing four opponents every week.

Richelieu passed a law banning duels in 1626. The punishment was death. The posh men were the ones who enjoyed a good duel most. One lord, Bouteville, decided to ignore the law and was caught. 'They won't dare execute me,' he thought.

He was beheaded. It was Bouteville's last duel – between the executioner's axe and his neck. Bouteville's neck lost.

Awful for animals

Humans have always been cruel to creatures, foul to fish, brutal to birds, rotten to reptiles and savage to sheep, sows, starlings, sardines and sausage dogs. You can bet they'd even have been deadly to dinosaurs if they'd been around. So it's no surprise to find the French were foul to their four-legged and feathered friends.

1 Blackbird blood Have you heard the nursery rhyme:

Sing a song of sixpence, a pocket full of rye,
Four and twenty blackbirds baked in a pie.
When the pie was opened the birds began to sing.
Wasn't that a dainty dish to set before a king?

A dainty dish lots of lords and ladies enjoyed. A crust was baked and songbirds popped underneath just before it was served. Good harmless fun. Unless the king was a French one in the Middle Ages. The French had an idea that was even more fun – they sent hawks to perch on the roof beams. When the birds flew out the hawks swooped down and destroyed them.

2 Suffering swans In the Middle Ages the French had a sport for July and August each year – swan catching. This was a chance for everyone, from the nobles and the churchmen to the peasants, to join together in tormenting young swans.

It was important that you went after swans that were too young to fly … after all, you wouldn't want them to have a chance to get away. This is what you do…

CHOOSE A POND OR CANAL WHERE THERE ARE LOTS OF YOUNG SWANS.

TEAMS HAVE A BOAT EACH AND SET OFF IN ORDER: PRIESTS FIRST, LORDS SECOND AND PEASANTS THIRD.

LIGHT YOUR WAY WITH FLAMING TORCHES AND HAVE LOTS OF LOUD MUSIC. CHASE THE YOUNG SWANS.

THE TEAM THAT CATCHES THE MOST SWANS IS THE WINNER. YOU ARE *NOT* ALLOWED TO KILL THE SWANS – JUST SCARE THE FEATHERS OFF THEM.

Fun? At other times, swans were killed and eaten. Their bodies were roasted then dressed in their feathers again. The beak and legs were stuck back on and covered in gold. The cooked bird was then placed on a river-bank scene made of sugar and painted pastry. This was placed on the dinner table for guests to admire ... then eat.

3 Slaughtered squirrels Animals were killed for their fur – they still are. But in the Middle Ages cute little squirrels were massacred in their millions to make posh folk's clothes.

Blanche de Bourbon went off to marry the Spanish king Pedro the Cruel in clothes made from the skins of 11,794 dead squirrels. Of course the squirrels would be pleased to know that her husband Pedro the Cruel was very ... cruel. Blanche and Pedro married in 1353, but Pedro fancied Maria de Padilla and he left Blanche soon after the marriage. Blanche was upset, but at least she had 11,794 dead squirrels to cheer her up.

4 Dreadful for dogs In the 1370s the villainous Charles of Navarre had an argument with the Count of Foix about some money. Charles gave the Count's son a bag of powder.

121

'Feed this magic powder to your father and we'll be friends again.' The Count of Foix found the powder and fed it to his dogs instead. The dogs howled in agony and died. Of course the powder was poison ... and of course the dogs were innocent. (The son was also innocent, of course, but he died horribly too. His father found the boy cleaning his nails with a knife. He grabbed him angrily, the knife slipped, the boy cut his own throat and died.)

Some dogs were luckier – Henry III used to carry a basket of small doggy pets with him. They were hung around his neck.

SMALL DOGGY PETS

5 Poor pigs In Dijon, in the Middle Ages, pigs wandered the streets looking for scraps of food. It was a hard life and they were tough pigs who learned to fight and bite for everything.

One pig ate a young child. The pig was put on trial for murder and was found guilty. Murderers in France were hanged – so they hanged the pig.

WHAT'S THE CHURCH'S POSITION ON EATING MURDERERS?

In 1740 a cow was hanged. Her crime? She was found guilty of being a witch.

6 Itchy insects Insects are often pests, of course, so people came up with jolly ways of getting rid of them. Goodman of Paris advised his wife…

Fleas

· You need:
    A loaf of bread
    A pot of glue
    A candle

· To use: Cover the bread in glue. Put the lighted candle on the top. The fleas will be attracted by the light and jump onto the loaf. The fleas will stick to the loaf. Burn the loaf.

He also suggested spreading a white woollen blanket on the floor. Fleas would be caught in the rough hairs and, because fleas are black and the wool is white, you can see the little pests and squash them.

Then there was his advice for trapping flies…

Flies

· You need:
A pot
A rag soaked in honey

· To use: Put the honey-rag in the bottom of the pot. Put the pot in the place that's plagued by flies. The flies will crawl into the pot. When the pot is full of flies, put the lid on and shake it. The flies' wings will stick to the rag and you can throw them out.

He had one last piece of good advice. If the fly trap didn't work … swat them.

7 Big sad wolf When wolves started to roam through Paris in 1439 they weren't so keen on the sheep or cows – they went for the shepherds. In November the biggest and most vicious wolf was finally killed. Its body was put in a wheelbarrow and the killers trundled it around Paris. They opened its jaws to show the fierce teeth and scare the kids. They also collected ten francs as a reward for their killing.

THIS'LL KEEP THE WOLF FROM THE DOOR

French kings hunted foxes for fun. But wimpy Henry IV didn't like getting wet. He had trees, grass and rocks brought into the palace, then a fox was set free and they hunted indoors.

8 Fat falcons It wasn't all bad news for animals and birds. Half a mile outside the walls of Paris was Montfaucon – or 'Falcon Hill'. How did it get its name? Because it was a popular place with falcons? They found lots of food there?

Yes, and no. The kind peasants of Paris didn't feed them tasty treats. The falcons ate the dead criminals who were executed there, or who were dumped there after being executed somewhere else, and left to rot.

Montfaucon was a mound five metres high and 10 x 12 metres in size. It had a platform in the middle and a 10-metre-high stone pillar at each corner. Beams of wood joined the four pillars and there was enough room to hang 60 people at a time.

There was a pit in the middle of the platform for the corpses. It was covered with a metal grating to stop the bones being stolen – but wide enough to let in the feasting falcons. Other bits of chopped or boiled bodies were hung there in wicker baskets for the people of Paris to peer at.

One criminal, Pierre des Essarts, was beheaded in 1413 but his body wasn't sent to his family for three years. There wasn't a lot left for them to bury by 1416.

9 Sad horses' tales In the 1600s and 1700s there were thousands of French people wandering the countryside, looking for work. As they drifted they often stopped to pinch chickens from farmyards, washing that was spread on hedges to dry, or milk from cows in the fields.

Sometimes they also sneaked up on horses and lopped off their tails. The horses had nothing to swish away flies.

What a rotten thing to do to a horse. Why on earth would they do that?

a) to knit the horse hair into a nice pair of socks

b) to sell to furniture makers for stuffing chairs

c) they were jealous of rich people who owned smart horses.

Answer: **b)** At least it didn't hurt the horse. Some of these travelling peasants also chopped themselves. They wanted to look like old war heroes when food and money was given out to soldiers.

10 Cruel for cats In the 1730s young Nicolas Contat was learning to be a printer in a Paris printer's shop. It was a miserable life living above the shop, with poor food and his sleep disturbed by howling alley cats.

Nicolas and his friends decided to get their own back on their lazy, bullying boss. They crawled into the roof and gave him a sample of what they suffered – they howled like cats and stopped him getting to sleep. At last the boss's wife said, 'Do anything but get rid of the cats around here – except for my lovely Big Grey, of course.'

The first thing Nicolas and his friends did was kill Big Grey, who used to get better food than they did.

Then they captured as many cats as they could and brought them into the printer's yard. The cats were given a trial by the boys, found guilty ... and hanged.

When the boss's wife saw the cats hanging in her yard she screamed for an hour. And the boys just laughed. Years later Nicolas Contat remembered the cat massacre as the happiest of his days in Paris!

It was a cruel world in those days but especially if you were a cat. Many holiday events used cruelty to cats as entertainment. They were...

- Set on fire and chased through the streets.
- Tied to a stake and burned like a witch.
- Tormented so their yowls made a hideous music.
- Put on top of a bonfire, a dozen in a basket.
- Bricked up (alive) into the walls of a new house for luck.

127

Evil eighteenth century

This was it. The big one. The century when all those practice revolutions finally paid off. Probably the most revolting century of all…

1729 The French are claiming a lot of land in America – Louisiana. Like the Brits they haven't asked the Native Americans. But when the French try to make Natchez Indians give up holy graveyards the Natchez massacre 300 French settlers. The French take revenge and the Natchez are almost wiped out by 1731.

1756 The Seven Years War starts. It's really all about who gets the wealth from the rich new lands in America. Will it be Britain or France? France loses almost all her lands in America and Canada. The French aren't happy so…

1775 France helps the American people to rebel – against their British rulers. America wins. Happy French! But France has taught her peasants an important lesson: revolution can succeed and you can get rid of your kings. So…

1789 The French Revolution begins. There have been poor harvests and starving peasants. This time the peasants will finally win a revolution. You can't say they don't deserve it after all those attempts.

1793 The French chop off their king's head – an idea they pinched from the English who did it 150 years before. But the French do a better job, because they also guillotine the Queen, many of the posh people (aristocrats) and anyone else who wants to pick a fight. This is 'The Terror' and it goes on for two years. Heads fall like raindrops. **1799** The French are fighting nearly everybody in the world. A great general steps forward and leads them to victory. He is Napoleon Bonaparte. The French are so grateful they will make him their Emperor … which is a bit like a king, really. Oh, dear. After finally getting rid of their monarchs what do they end up with a few years later? A monarch.

Revolutionary rottenness

In 1789 the French peasants were starving – again. An Englishman, Arthur Young, visited France and was shocked…

Many of the ploughmen and their wives have no shoes or stockings. The children look hungry. Their clothes are so ragged they may as well not have any. I saw one little girl whose only toy was a stick. It made my heart ache to see her.

The English writer, Tobias Smollett, had described the peasants a few years earlier…

They are more like starved scarecrows than human beings.

NOW THAT'S SCARY

The taxes were high. Poor peasants tried to farm their own land then go out to work for the rich farmers to make extra money. They had to do two jobs just to scrape a miserable living.

One unfair tax was collected for the local lord's pigeons – the peasants had to give their corn to feed them. (This is a bit like every pupil in a class having to give teacher a litre of petrol so he can drive his Rolls Royce to school while they walk. Now that would cause a revolution!)

King Louis wasn't too popular and the rebels really hated Queen Marie Antoinette because she seemed to spend a fortune while they starved.

What do French kings do when the peasants rebel? Send in the soldiers. But this time something odd happened.

King Louis XVI kept a diary. On the day the trouble started he wrote just one word…

14 July 1789

Nothing

How wrong could one king be?

If the French Revolution had kept a diary it might have looked something like this…

Diary of a revolution

May 1789

France is in a mess. Going broke in fact. So King Louis <u>XVI</u> calls the Church, the Lords and the common people (the three 'Estates') to meet and sort it out. But the common people, the Third Estate, want all the power and some of the First Estate, the priests, join them.

18 June 1789

Now the common people call themselves 'The National Assembly'. The King is upset and has them locked out of their meeting hall. The National Assembly don't need his smelly meeting hall. They just meet at an indoor tennis court instead. They say, 'We are going to stay here till we get the changes we want.' They are getting stroppy, aren't they?

14 July 1789

It's my birthday! Today the French Revolution was born. Of course, I've been on the way for a thousand years, but today I arrived at last.

And what a day it's been! It started when a Paris mob headed for the 'Hôtel des Invalides' to get weapons. The King's troops, led by Baron de Besenval, faced the mob. Besenval gave the order...

Charge!

... and the troops said...

No!

The soldiers didn't just refuse to fight the mob — they joined them and marched on the royal prison, the Bastille, to get more guns and gunpowder. The Bastille guards tried to defend the prison. A hundred of the mob died when guards fired at them, but in the end they broke in and freed the prisoners ... all seven of them.

The French Revolution has started. Happy birthday to me.

August 1789

The people of Paris are happy – makes a change. The King has agreed to impove things and the people love him – makes a change.

But in the rest of France the peasants are NOT happy bunnies because they have no food and no jobs – this does not make a change. They are making trouble, stealing their lords' deer and shooting their doves, raiding the posh people's fishponds

and even burning down their houses.
  Gangs of robbers roam the country roads just like in the bad old days of the Hundred Years War. Then food riots spread back to Paris again. The King's minister, Foullon de Doué is supposed to have said...

If the peasants are hungry they can eat hay

He was captured and given a necklace of nettles, a bunch of thistles was stuffed into his tied hands and hay was stuffed into his mouth. Then he was hanged from a lamp-post.

October 1789
  The people of Paris decided they wanted the King in Paris where they could keep their eye on him. (They were worried he'd send his troops to flatten them again.) So today

thousands of people just marched to his palace at Versailles. It was a ten-mile walk in the rain. The rebels arrived, tired, wet, angry and hungry.

King Louis and Queen Marie Antoinette tried to flee in their coach – daft idea – of course the rebels just stopped them.

It's Marie Antoinette that the rebel mob really hates. The threats were blood-curdling. Some of the cries were...

Cut her throat and tear her skin for hair-ribbons

Wring her neck – tear her heart out

Fry her liver

I'll eat her lungs

I'll have her guts

And I'll have her kidneys cooked in wine

The Queen was a bit worried. But they daren't touch her – yet.

Early next morning the starving rebels killed a horse and roasted it over an open fire. Now they had the courage to march into the royal palace and capture their King and his hated Queen.

One of the Queen's bodyguards tried to stop them. He was stabbed with pikes till he fell. The mob dragged him out to the courtyard where a man with a pointed hat stood over him, raised an axe and sliced off his head.

The head was raised on a pole and led the procession back to Paris. The King, Queen, Prince and Princess of France were put in a coach and forced to go to Paris.

Tonight the peasants of France have their King and Queen as prisoners. What will they do with them?

> *14 July 1790*
>
> *Happy birthday to me. The crowds in Paris celebrate with a party. The King and Queen are invited and the people cheer them. What a nice peaceful revolution I am turning out to be...*

The great escape

The imprisoned King and Queen needed a way out. King Louis hatched a plan:

FIRST WE RUN AWAY FROM PARIS AND THE MOB. THEN WE GET THE OTHER KINGS OF EUROPE TO LEND US THEIR ARMIES AND WE FIGHT BACK!

GREAT! MY BROTHER IS EMPEROR OF AUSTRIA. HE'LL HELP

But the kings of Europe didn't want to help – except for potty King Gustav of Sweden.

Of course, running off and getting foreign armies to fight the French people would upset the French people. Can you blame them? It was 'treason'. And the punishment for treason was death.

And, anyway, the plan to escape was a disaster. If the Paris people had had a popular newspaper in those days the story would have made front-page headlines...

One sou

Paris Post

Wednesday
22 June 1791

CRIMINAL KING CAUGHT IN COACH
Austrian she-dog queen caught too

Today King Louis and his Austrian witch of a queen were caught trying to escape. They were fleeing to Austria in an attempt to stab France in the back.

Disguise

On Monday 20 June the foul royal family acted all day as if nothing was happening. At four in the afternoon the wicked queen even walked her children in the public parks as she did most days. At nine the royal brats went to bed as usual. But at ten she woke them and the traitorous two put their plan into action.

First Prince Louis was dressed in a girl's dress as a disguise. The rotten royal family slipped into a disused part of the Tuileries Palace and out to a waiting coach where they sent their children off safely. Count Axel Fersen, dressed as a coachman, held open the door. Everyone knows that the crafty Count is in fact the Queen's not-so-secret boyfriend.

Escape carriage

The Queen went back and disguised herself in a plain grey dress and a veil to hide her famous face. As she stepped out of the Palace door she saw one of the gallant guards pacing up and down. As soon as he turned his back she ran out to where her guide was waiting. But the guide got lost and

138

had to ask passing Paris people for directions. At last the Queen reached the safety of her escape carriage.

Sneaking Queen

Meanwhile, back in the Palace, King Louis disguised himself under a large dark wig and a round hat. He left in a separate coach.

Clear of Paris

When the royals reached the Paris boundary around 2:00 a.m. they had a stroke of good luck. The guards were having a party and took little notice of the runaway royals. By daylight they were well clear of Paris.

They were recognized in the town of Sainte-Menehould

and the local guard set off after them. The royals reached Varennes but couldn't find the inn where they were supposed to change horses. By then it was close to midnight. King Louis climbed down and knocked on the door of the nearest house. The reply from the owner of the house was, 'Clear off!' The Queen tried and got an even ruder answer.

Arrested

That was when the royals drove back into the town centre – and into the waiting muskets of the guards from Sainte-Menehould. A grocer called Sauce was acting as chief guard and he asked to see their passports – faked, of course. Even then they might have escaped if it hadn't been for the stupid she-dog Marie Antoinette. She was supposed to be a humble servant but when guard Sauce looked at her passport she snapped, 'Hurry up, will you?' No humble servant would ever speak like that. Sauce arrested them.

Civic Sauce

The royal family spent Tuesday night in the Sauce home. The royal children were stuck in bed with the little Sauce children.

The grocer asked, 'Are you the King of France?'

'Certainly not,' Louis lied.

'I have a friend who worked at your Versailles Palace,' Sauce said sharply. 'I'll send for him.'

And, when the friend arrived, he bowed before Louis. 'Oh, all right, I'm the King,' Louis admitted.

This evening the family are on their way back to Paris. Long-faced Louis was heard to mutter, 'There is no longer a King of France.'

Captured King

Too right, Louis. You've betrayed your people and you don't deserve to rule us. The end is close for you.

God save France!

The journey back to Paris was grim. The peasants had really turned against the royal family now. They spat at the King and tore the Queen's clothes. Furious gangs jumped on the carriage, wild women swore at the royal family.

But Paris was curiously calm. Messages were scrawled on the walls of the city...

King Louis and Queen Marie Antoinette were driven through the dusty Paris streets in an eerie silence.

Rescuing the royals

Louis and Marie Antoinette had failed in their escape plan, but all wasn't lost ... they thought. If Marie's nephew, the new Emperor of Austria, invaded France then the Austrians would set her free.

The trouble was the Austrians sent a message to the French people which was a bit violent. It more or less said...

Of course the people of Paris read this and said…

The posh people of Paris gathered at Louis and Marie's Palace. Three hundred arrived to defend him. Some were armed with swords but others were only armed with shovels. Some just brought pokers and tongs from the fireside, but all were ready to die defending their king. Brave? Or just stupid?

The King surrendered to the Assembly and told his guard to surrender or they would be massacred. His 500 guards put down their weapons … and the revolutionaries massacred them anyway. (That's cheating.)

A horrible rampage of murdering followed...

- The mob rushed into the Palace and killed everyone they found – even maidservants.
- Some servants and nobles ran into the gardens and climbed the statues. The mob didn't fire muskets in case they damaged the statues. They hacked down the victims with pikes then stabbed them.
- Some very young boys were found playing football in the Palace garden ... with human heads.

King Louis and Queen Marie Antoinette were thrown in prison – which is a little bit better than being massacred.

Did you know...?

The French Revolution wasn't good for the leaders of the French Army. During the war with Austria the Duke de Biron ordered, 'Charge the enemy with your bayonets!'

His soldiers replied, 'Hang on! We are free and equal. We'll have a vote.' They voted, 'Non! We don't want to.'

No wonder the war went badly.

The bloody royal end

The King and Queen were in prison. They thought they still might be rescued by the invading Austrians and that kept their hopes high. But once the blood began to flow there was only going to be one end. A bloody one.

1 By 3 September 1792 the war was going badly. The French were losing. They couldn't kill the Austrian invaders ... so they started killing off the French people they didn't trust. As revolutionary leader Marat said...

Let the blood of the traitors flow. It is the only way to save France.

Blood of the posh people was top of the list, of course.

One of the Queen's friends met a nasty end. The royal family were sitting down to dinner in their prison when they heard a racket. Guards and common people burst into the room…

LOOK OUT OF THE WINDOW, YOUR MAJESTIES, AND SEE WHAT HAPPENS TO THE LIKES OF YOU

NO, DON'T LOOK!

The royals looked out anyway. Some people were waving a pole at the window. On the pole was a head. Its long fair hair was caked with blood and waved in the wind. They recognized it. Marie Antoinette cried as she fainted…

THE PRINCESS DE LAMBALLE! MY FRIEND!

The unlucky princess had been beheaded. Her body was dragged through the streets while the head was perched on a pole. Her heart had been ripped out and waved on the end of a sword.

2 Louis XVI was executed on 20 January 1793. He died horribly. He was laid face down on the guillotine and the executioner, Sanson, pulled the rope.

The blade fell.

The King screamed. His neck was so fat the blade failed to slice it off first time. It came off at a second attempt.

A young guard, about 18 years old, picked up the head for the crowd to see. 'Long live the Revolution!' they cried. They rushed forward to dip handkerchiefs in the blood.

3 In October 1793 Marie Antoinette was given a joke trial – everyone knew they were going to sentence her to death. The Queen went to her death quite bravely, but her guards didn't treat her too kindly...

- They arrived in her cell and insisted on tying her hands behind her back. 'The King didn't have his hands tied when you executed him!' she argued. They tied her anyway. They then had to untie her again so she could have a pee.
- They chopped her hair so it wouldn't get in the way of the guillotine.
- She was put into a cart and led through the streets of Paris.
- She was tied to the end of a rope and the executioner held the other end.
- The guillotine was supposed to be quick – a couple of people a minute could be chopped. Yet it took them four long, fear-filled minutes to prepare Marie Antoinette.

- As she stepped on to the platform she trod on the foot of the exeutioner and the wimpy man cried out in pain. So Marie Antoinette's famous last words were…

I beg your pardon, Sir, I didn't do it on purpose.

- The executioner removed her white cap. It showed that she was almost bald. The crowd laughed and jeered at her.
- The blade came down, the head fell. A revolutionary picked up the head and waved it at the cheering crowd.

I HATE CROWDS

The Terror – 1792

There was no real law and order by autumn 1792. Gangs of revolutionaries set up their own courts, tried people and had them butchered. These 'legal' bloodbaths became known as 'terrors'. Here are some of the most horrible happenings in the September 1792 massacres, when mobs broke into the prisons and killed the prisoners…

1 Priests who failed to help the Revolution were cut down with swords. A prisoner watched the killing and reported:

> *The priests who tried to protect themselves with their hands suffered most because the blows were weak when they reached the head. Some lost hands or arms before they fell. We told each other the quickest death was to stand with your hands behind your back.*

2 A prisoner tried to escape up a chimney. The judge told the jailer…

> *If he escapes then we'll execute you in his place. Fire shots up the chimney.*

When the shots failed they lit a straw fire in the hearth. The choking prisoner fell down and was killed.

3 Women helped to load the bodies on to carts so they could be taken away to be buried. They often took breaks to dance on the blood-soaked ground. Many of them sliced off the ears of bodies and pinned them to their aprons.

4 Not many of the victims were noblemen. Most were just common thieves and beggars. Twelve hundred people died in the autumn of 1792 – and 37 of them were women. There were less than 200 executioners doing the dirty work.

5 One executioner cut out the heart of a nobleman and squeezed the blood into a wine glass. He told a girl, 'Drink this or your father in prison will die.' What would *you* do if someone offered you that threat? What did *she* do?

Answer: She drank it.

147

6 The executioners were mainly ordinary people like shop-keepers. They executed people then they took their bloody axes back to their shops and hung them up so everyone could see what good revolutionaries they were.

A few years later the massacres of September 1792 started to disgust most French people. The executioners came up with another story…

ACTUALLY I LIED ABOUT EXECUTING PEOPLE. I JUST DIPPED MY AXE IN A BUCKET OF BUTCHER'S BLOOD AND PRETENDED. I'M A NICE MAN REALLY

Meanwhile the Minister of Justice, Georges Jacques Danton, shrugged and said…

I don't give a damn for the prisoners. Let them look after themselves.

You may be pleased to know that, two years later, deadly Danton became a prisoner and went for a guillotine chop.

The Terror – 1793

In October 1793 a new Terror began when one lot of revolutionaries (the Jacobins) began to execute another lot of revolutionaries (the Girondins).

The choppers were chopped. Here are five foul headlines about the Terror … only the key words are missing. Can you fill them in?

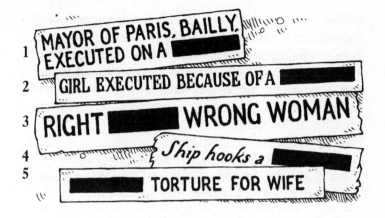

1 MAYOR OF PARIS, BAILLY, EXECUTED ON A ▆▆▆▆

2 GIRL EXECUTED BECAUSE OF A ▆▆▆▆

3 RIGHT ▆▆▆▆ WRONG WOMAN

4 *Ship hooks a*

5 ▆▆▆▆ TORTURE FOR WIFE

Missing words are: husband, name, dance, pair of corpses, rubbish tip.

Answers:

1 Rubbish tip. The guillotine was taken to pieces and carried to a Paris rubbish tip for Bailly's execution. That's how much the people hated their old mayor.

2 Dance. A girl who danced with an enemy soldier was beheaded for the 'crime'.

3 Name. A woman was arrested and taken to court. 'Yes, that is my name, but I am not the woman you want. You want a woman with the same name in the next street.' The judge just said, 'We have you here so we'll try you instead.' She was executed.

4 Pair of corpses. At Nantes the guillotine was too slow. So executioners chained prisoners together, put them in barges, and sank them in the River Loire. Sometimes sailing ships that put down anchors would pull up the anchor with bodies hooked on them.

HOW'S THE FISHING?

5 Husband. A woman cried when she saw her husband executed. Her punishment was to die by beheading. But for a couple of hours she had to lie on the guillotine while her husband's headless body was allowed to drip blood over her. Then the blade put her out of her misery. Nasty.

The gruesome guillotine

The secret of speedy slicing was a machine that could kill kings cleanly and queens quickly, and lop lords and ladies like lightning. The guillotine.

Foul guillotine facts

1 The first French guillotine was built by Dr Joseph Guillotin ... but he had advice on how to build it. Who advised him? King Louis XVI. Imagine that. What must he have been thinking as he laid his head on the machine?

2 Chopping French aristo heads started before the guillotines were built. The first day of the Revolution was 14 July 1789. On that day one nobleman, the Marquis of Launay, the governor of the Bastille, was caught by a Paris mob who cut off his head with a knife. His followers suffered the same charming chopping and their heads were paraded around Paris. The guillotine didn't replace the knife for another three years.

3 The guillotine is a famous machine of the French Revolution … but head-chopping machines had been invented 200 years before. One was used in Halifax, northern England, to execute cattle thieves and one was used in Scotland when the Earl of Morton was executed on it in 1581. The Scots called it 'The Maiden'. Dr Guillotin pinched the English and Scottish idea.

4 The guillotine was quick, and good executioners could get through two victims a minute. Not easy.

5 The head shooting off from the guillotine became known as 'sneezing into the basket'. Atch-ouch. The guillotine itself was known as what?

a) The Red Theatre?
b) The People's Avenger?
c) The National Razor?

OH, WELL I NEEDED A SHAVE

Answer: All three.

6 The guillotine was tested first on live sheep and calves, then on dead bodies. Finally it was tried out on a live highwayman called Pelletier. Crowds turned out on 25 April 1792 to watch his execution. They went away grumbling, 'It was all over so quickly. It was no fun at all.' They marched off singing…

BRING ME BACK MY HANGING TREE

151

7 The French Revolution Terror from 1792 to 1794 sliced lots of heads off in two years – but the St Bartholomew's Day Massacre in 1572 killed more in one DAY.

8 One woman made a living by making wax masks from the dead heads in the guillotine basket. Her name was Madame Tussaud. Nice job.

9 Dr Guillotin invented the guillotine because he was such a *kind* man! He didn't want criminals to suffer. He said all they'd feel would be a tickle at the back of the neck. Oh yeah? Care to try it and prove it? One victim who felt *nothing* was called Valaze. He stabbed himself to death in court in 1793 – but the judge said his corpse had to be guillotined anyway.

10 Some French doctors took a front seat at the executions to test if the head lived on after the chop. When the head fell they called out the victim's name. One reported...

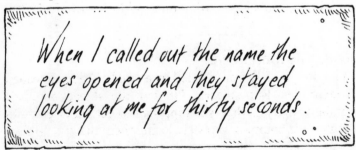

When I called out the name the eyes opened and they stayed looking at me for thirty seconds.

That's nonsense (you'll be pleased to know if you are ever sent to the guillotine).

Happy ending 1?

It's said Dr Guillotin's cousin, also called Guillotin, helped him to design the killing machine. But then he had to watch as the woman he loved lost her head on their invention. Cousin Guillotin turned against the executioners and worked for their enemies – the people who wanted a King of France again. This was treason – Cousin Guillotin was arrested and executed. How? With the guillotine, of course.

Happy ending 2?

France's chief guillotine executioner was Charles-Henri Sanson. He was good at his job and once executed 300 men and women in three days. He wasn't keen on executing women and he did not enjoy executing King Louis XVI – but he didn't dare refuse.

It was a tricky job, high up on the blood-soaked platform. One day Charles-Henri's son, Gabriel, was helping Dad to dead-head the traitors. Gabriel slipped, fell off the platform and crashed to the cobbled street below. Gabriel died. After that a fence was put up round the guillotine platform.

The last public execution on a guillotine was in 1939.

Ratty Robespierre

The 'Reign of Terror' was led by a weedy little man called Maximilien Robespierre. He led the department for 'Public Safety' – that was supposed to get rid of enemies of France. Enemies who were losing them the war. In time it started to get rid of enemies of Robespierre.

No one was safe. In the end everyone in government was so scared of Robespierre they ganged up on him and had him arrested with his gang of bullies. Robespierre was signing a letter calling in the army to kill his enemies. That's when a man named Charles-André Merda took a hand. He described his gallant attack on Robespierre's lair…

28 July 1794

The staircase was filled with Robespierre's supporters. I could hardly get through. I was very excited. Robespierre's gang were in the main room and all the passages to it were closed off. I pretended I was a messenger with a secret message. I reached the door of their room. At last it was opened. There were about fifty people in there. I recognised Robespierre in the middle of them. I leapt at him and pointed a sword at his heart and cried, 'Surrender you traitor!' He looked up and said, 'It is you

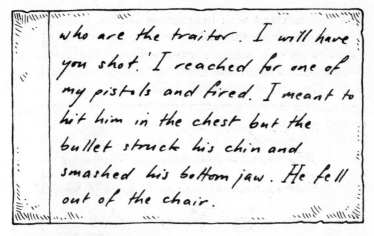

who are the traitor. I will have you shot.' I reached for one of my pistols and fired. I meant to hit him in the chest but the bullet struck his chin and smashed his bottom jaw. He fell out of the chair.

Merda was a bit of a liar, but this part of the story was probably close to the truth. Robespierre had been about to sign the order that would set the army loose on the people of Paris. The paper has 'Ro …' at the bottom and splashes of blood on it.

Robespierre's gang had sent hundreds to the guillotine. Now it was their bloodstained turn…

- Robespierre's brother, Augustin, tried to escape by jumping from a window. He broke his leg and was caught. Chop!

- Couthon fell down some stairs in his effort to get away and gashed his forehead. He went to the guillotine bandaged. Chop!

- Hanriot was thrown out of a window – but survived because he fell on a rubbish heap. Soldiers found him and tore out one eye which was left hanging down his cheek. As he climbed onto the guillotine the following evening a spectator snatched the eye off. Chop!

- Robespierre was patched up by a doctor so he was still alive when he went to the guillotine. The executioner tore off the bandage and his jaw almost fell away. A witness said, 'He let out a groan like a dying tiger. Everyone in the square heard it.' It didn't hurt for long. Chop!

A woman screamed at Robespierre...

> *Go to your grave with the curses of the wives and mothers of France. Your death makes me drunk with happiness.*

Over 80 of Robespierre's supporters followed him for the chop. In many parts of France the leaders of the Terror were executed and the worst of the Terror was over.

Who suffered most? Surprise, surprise, the poor peasants.

- The price of bread rose and they starved. The people who had bread made fortunes. They ate at restaurants where a meal cost as much as a peasant made in two months.
- In early 1795 freezing weather froze the rivers and wolves came down from the hills to attack people and their animals.
- The spring thaw made the rivers flood their homes and fields.

After the Terror

Of course the peasants revolted. Not against a king now, but against their own government. Even in tragic times like these, history has its horribly hideous human moments.

On 20 May 1795 the poor people marched on the government. They broke down the doors to tell their Members of Parliament what they thought of them.

Time for a hero to step forward – and it was young Jean Féraud. He threw himself down in front of the mob and cried…

The rebels marched to the President's seat. Féraud dusted himself down and rushed to the defence … again.

Féraud's body was kicked out of the building and a local innkeeper sliced off the head 'like topping a turnip' (a witness said). Then the rebels stuck the head on a pike and carried it back in to show the President.

After 1,000 years of revolution the kings had gone – but the poor were still starving and the rebels were still as vicious as ever. That's what hunger and spite does to you. After 1,000 years the French hadn't learned a lot.

Song of a revolution

The French have the world's best national anthem – written in 1792, before they'd executed their King and when enemies were invading France...

Can't you hear the roar of his cruel soldiers across the country?
They are coming to butcher your friends and family.
Citizens, take up arms, form your regiments and march.
Wash the fields with their evil blood!

Great, blood-stirring stuff.

But *before* that was written the French peasants had their own rebel song. This is not so well known – but just as gruesome. Next time you lead a rebellion (against cruel school exams or crueller school dinners) you'll need a good song to march to. Try the French Revolution one...

We Will Win

Let us sing for joy, because the good times
they are coming;
We common folk were nobodies but now
we're really something.

Chorus: We will win, we will win, we will
win; The people of this day will always sing,
We will win, we will win, we will win;
In spite of the traitors, we will win.

We'll string up all the nobles from the
lampposts, wait and see!
The lords and ladies all must die to give us
liberty.

The nobles all will die and we'll be free of
priests as well,
The vicars and their bishops they will all be
sent to Hell.

Little Boney

What did the rulers of France do when the peasants revolted? They sent in the army, every time.

In 1795 the army was winning battles but this was a tough job. So it was time for the government to turn to a bright young general – the 26-year-old Napoleon Bonaparte.

Boney was a little bloke. He had good points and bad points...

- Good: he'd always supported the Revolution.
- Bad: he'd also supported the rotten Robespierre.
- Good: he'd fought well as a captain at Toulon against enemies of the Revolution.
- Bad: he'd then ducked out of fighting a nasty little war in the west.

Napoleon hung round Paris, whingeing about how unfairly the government was treating him. He was a shabby, long-haired little figure, wandering the streets of Paris and threatening to kill himself, when government minister Barras sent for him and said...

WILL YOU LEAD THE GOVERNMENT FORCES? YOU HAVE JUST THREE MINUTES TO DECIDE

Boney agreed. The rebels outnumbered the government forces. Boney had a tough job on his hands. He lined up his men and waited for the rebel attack.

He then did something the rebels didn't really expect – something which would make him a great leader. He fought dirty.

On 5 October 1795 at 3pm the rebels marched towards Boney firing their muskets – Boney's men fired back with cannons. The rebels were blown away. By 6pm the rebellion – and probably the French Revolution – was over.

Boney boss

Napoleon was made chief of the French army in Italy. Once he started winning, the French government couldn't stop him going on and on. He ended up in Egypt.

Napoleon's army was trapped in Egypt when Britain's Admiral Nelson was sinking the French army ships. So Napoleon left his army there and sneaked home alone. He was a deserter. How would the people of Paris treat a deserter?

The French welcomed him home like a hero. The people were a bit fed up with the government and the Revolution by then. What they wanted was a strong leader … someone like Napoleon in fact.

On 9 November 1799 Napoleon marched into the French Parliament with the army of Paris. The Members of Parliament ran away. Napoleon was made leader with two other men. But five years later he was top man. Emperor of France.

The Revolution had got rid of a king – and replaced him with an emperor.

A little change – a lot of blood.

Nasty nineteenth century

The terrors of the Revolution were over but France was still a dangerous and deadly place to live throughout the 1800s. After the Revolution of 1789, and all the bloodshed of the Terrors and Napoleon's wars, France had a king again! But how long would it last?

It seemed that bits of French history were being acted out again – and again – and again.

1814 Boney beaten. Louis XVIII (brother of chopped Louis XVI) takes the throne.

1824 Louis XVIII died and another brother, Charles X, is king.

1830 Charlie X upsets Parliament and they force him to chuck in the crown. But they just give the throne to another feller, Louis Philippe. Lou-Phil upsets lots of people too but he manages to hang on for 18 years in spite of attempts to assassinate him.

1848 Most of Europe seems to be revolting and the French aren't going to be left out. There are the usual food shortages so the peasants rebel – and suffer mass execution at the hands of the government. France decides it can get along without kings (again). The new government is a 'Republic' – like the one they had in 1793 when Louis XVI got the chop. They also get themselves a President – Louis Napoleon, nephew of Napoleon Bonaparte.

1849 Louis gets rid of the Republic

and makes himself Emperor Napoleon III.

1870 Napoleon III gets into a war with Germany (the Franco-Prussian War) and loses it. He is forced to pack his bags (and crown) and go. The people of Paris rise up against their own Republican government. They call themselves

'Communards' and surprise, surprise, they are massacred by the army.

Boney's war

Napoleon Bonaparte became Emperor of France in 1804. And Napoleon picked fights with everyone else in Europe. Yep – another l–o–n–g war.

Wars cost money. France had a huge amount of land in America that stretched from the Mississippi River to the Rockies. In 1803 Napoleon sold it to the United States for 15 million dollars. (No one bothered to ask the Native Americans who lived there, of course.)

Now Napoleon could have some really good battles...

NAPOLEON'S STORY

1805

NAPOLEON DECIDES TO INVADE BRITAIN - BUT THE BRITISH NAVY IS TOO STRONG. BRIT ADMIRAL NELSON SMASHES FRENCH AT TRAFALGAR - BUT IS SHOT. MANAGES A FEW FAMOUS LAST WORDS...

Thank God I have done my duty.

SO NAP STICKS TO LAND BATTLES AND SMASHES THE AUSTRIANS AND RUSSIANS AT ·AUSTERLITZ. 26,000 DEAD

THANK GOD YOU HAVE DONE YOUR DUTY

WHERE HAVE I HEARD THAT BEFORE?

1806

NAPOLEON FIGHTS PRUSSIANS AT JENA BUT A BRAIN ILLNESS MEANS HE SLEEPS THROUGH THE BATTLE

THANK GOD I HAVE DONE MY ZZZZZZZZZ

1808

FRENCH TRYING TO CONQUER SPAIN SO THE BRITS SEND AN ARMY TO HELP THE SPANISH. WITHOUT NAPOLEON TO LEAD THEM THE FRENCH DON'T DO SO WELL IN SPAIN BUT...

1810

...FRENCH RULE MOST OF EUROPE. NAPOLEON TELLS HIS BROTHER HIS BIG SECRET...

I reign through the fear I bring.

1812

AT BORODINO IN RUSSIA, NAPOLEON HAS A BAD BLADDER WHICH MAKES RIDING PAINFUL. STILL HE LOOKS AT THE CORPSES AND SAYS...

It is the most beautiful battlefield I have ever seen.

FRENCH WIN THAT BATTLE BUT THE RUSSIAN WINTER FREEZES THEM AND THEY HAVE TO GO HOME. 380,000 FRENCH DIE OF THE COLD AND HUNGER AND DISEASE

1813

NAPOLEON'S BAD GUT (COLIC AND A STOMACH ULCER) MAKES HIM ALMOST TOO ILL TO COMMAND AT DRESDEN

HE'S GOT A DICKY TUMMY

POOR GUY

THEN THE FRENCH FIGHT RUSSIANS, PRUSSIANS, SWEDES AND AUSTRIANS AND LOSE AT LEIPZIG. NAPOLEON FALLS ASLEEP (AGAIN) AND CAN'T ORGANIZE RETREAT. SO FRENCH ARMY SMASHED. 60,000 FRENCH LOST

YAWN - HAS ANYTHING INTERESTING HAPPENED?

1814
NAPOLEON GIVES UP AND GOES OFF TO THE ISLAND OF ELBA. KING LOUIS XVIII (BROTHER OF CHOPPED LOUIS XVI) TAKES THE THRONE

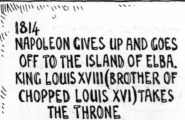

I GUESS YOU'RE HEAD OF THE COUNTRY NOW

I WISH YOU WOULDN'T USE THE WORD 'HEAD'

1815
NAPOLEON COMES BACK TO FRANCE FOR ONE LAST TRY BUT THEN HE MEETS THE BRITS AT WATERLOO

HOW DO YOU DO?

FINE THANKS, AND YOU?

NAPOLEON SUFFERING FROM 'PILES' (A SORE BUM) CAN HARDLY BEAR TO SIT ON HIS HORSE

FRENCH LOSE TO BRITS, LED BY THE DUKE OF WELLINGTON. NAPOLEON CAPTURED. END OF WAR

WELLINGTON'S BOOT

BONAPARTE'S BOT

NAPOLEON SENT TO THE ISLAND OF ST HELENA. NO ESCAPE EXCEPT...

1821
...THROUGH HIS DEATH. FAMOUS LAST WORDS?

Chief of the army

Nobbling Napoleon

But did Napoleon die saying something more exciting? Something like…

I'VE BEEN MURDERED!

…because that's what most historians now believe. A newspaper report of 2001 summed it up…

 YESTERDAY'S NEWS

HORRIBLE HISTORY MYSTERY
WHO KILLED BONAPARTE?

There are many people today who admire French dictator Napoleon and they believe he was murdered. But they don't believe he was killed by his English captors on the island of St Helena. Amazingly the fans of Napoleon think the ex-Emperor was murdered by his French countrymen.

They believe he was murdered slowly with arsenic poisoning. There are 31 signs of arsenic poison and in the last four years of his life Napoleon suffered 28 of them, including:

• a hatred of bright light
• rib pain
• loss of hair and teeth
• vomiting and diarrhoea
• discoloured nails
• sleeping problems

ST HELENA

The chief suspect is one of Bonaparte's companions, the French aristocrat, Charles Montholon. He had plenty of chances to slip the Emperor the poison but why would he want to? Montholon was a friend to Napoleon – but he was also short of money.

Montholon – murderer?

It is quite likely the French government paid Charles Montholon to do the deed. After all, France was settling down under her new king and they didn't want Napoleon returning and bringing more war and misery – that's what he'd done when he escaped from the island of Elba back in 1815.

Another historian believes Montholon only wanted to make Napoleon a bit sick so they would both be sent back to France.

Whatever the reason, one thing seems certain. Napoleon had arsenic in his body when he died. Recent USA tests on a lock of the Emperor's hair prove that.

So the mighty ruler of Europe was murdered. Whodunit? We can never be certain, but the finger of suspicion points at the French royal family who didn't want the great man to return ... ever.

Nineteenth-century nonsense

Here are a few fascinating facts for you to bring up at the school dinner table – and some of them may make your mates bring up their school dinners! Entertain everyone and become the most popular person at lunch – just turn to the person next to you and say: 'It's strange, but true…'

The three men were accused of plotting against Louis XVIII, the 'father' of the French people. And the punishment for attacking a father was to have a hand cut off. So the men had a hand chopped and then were taken to the guillotine to have their heads off too. Splat.

Giuseppe had been a soldier with Napoleon and he hated kings. In July 1835 he decided to assassinate King Louis Philippe. He rigged up 25 guns to fire together when he pulled the string. That way he could kill the King and his sons as they walked down the street.

He missed King Lou-Phil and the sons but killed 18 other people including a girl of 12. He was executed … with just a single guillotine chop. Splat.

In 1840 Louis tried to copy Uncle Napoleon Bonaparte and landed with a small force. He expected the rest of the

French to join him. They didn't have time. His little army was nearly drowned in the Boulogne surf as they tried to land. He was rescued by the Boulogne soldiers – who arrested him. The invasion lasted three hours and 20 minutes. And the vulture? The sign of Napoleon was an eagle – but Louis Nap couldn't get his hands on one so he took a vulture in a cage instead. In France Louis was caged – but not executed. No splat.

In 1858 Felice Orsini (an Italian) threw a bomb at Napoleon III as the Emperor drove to the opera. Napoleon survived but eight people in the street died and another 100 were injured. Felice's friends in London made the bomb for him. The French were a bit upset with the British after this. Felice was executed, of course. Splat.

A 14-year-old girl, Bernadette Soubirous, said…

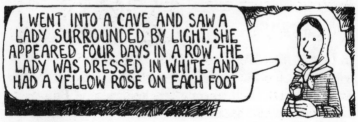

It was a miracle and pilgrims began going to her town of Lourdes to see for themselves. And today they're still going to find a miracle cure for sickness. They paddle in the water in the cave. Splash.

The Communard rebels of 1871 weren't very clear about what they wanted. But they did know they wanted so many public toilets in Paris that no one would ever have to pee in the Paris streets again. Splash.

In 1894 Santo Caserio walked up to President Sadi-Carnot with a bunch of flowers. The President's guards let Santo through and the killer draw a knife and stab the President. Caserio chopped. Splat!

Paris shops in the nineteenth century sold small pistols that fired perfume when you pulled the trigger. A bit like a water pistol today only more smelly. Splash.

In 1870 Germany invaded France and surrounded Paris. The people in the trapped city starved and had to eat cats and dogs and rats. In the end they went to Paris zoo, killed the elephant and ate it. Probably made it into jumbo-burgers. Splat.

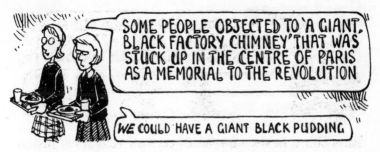

And it's still there today. The 'giant black factory chimney' is the Eiffel Tower, of course. The 289-metre tower[1] was built in 1889 for the 100th birthday of the Revolution so people would remember the great event.

1 Other books tend to disagree over the recorded height of the tower, but the figure 289 was meant to refer to the date of the Revolution in 1789.

173

Epilogue

The days of blood spilling on French fields wasn't over, of course. In the twentieth century France was at the bleeding heart of two dreadful world wars. But that's another story for another book.

The French Revolution was one of the great events in history. Ordinary people changed their world. Of course it took 1,000 years of misery and practising in smaller revolts to stir them into real action. But the peasants rebelled and wiped out so many lords and ladies that they got rid of them for years and years.

As an American rebel, Thomas Jefferson, said,

The tree of liberty must be watered from time to time with the blood of leaders. It is its natural manure.

(Of course Jefferson went on to become the third US president. Did he change his mind about shedding blood of leaders when he became one? Probably.)

He also said…

A little rebellion now and then is a good thing.

And he may be right. The French had lots of 'little rebellions' through their history – but nothing much changed for the better for the poor people until 1789. So sometimes people commit vicious and bloody acts to win their freedom. Heads were chopped, and chopping a head is a brutal business. And sometimes it wasn't left to soldiers or executioners to give the final chop…

When the people of Paris captured the Bastille prison on 14 July 1789 they took the governor prisoner. It wasn't a butcher who cut off the governor's hated head – it was a cook. And it wasn't as quick and clean as a guillotine. The whole happening was messy. A mob of people – including a boy just eight years old – took the governor of the Bastille alive. But…

175

History is made up of messy scuffles like that. A murder caused by a cook's kick. How angry do you have to be to do that? The French people had 1,000 years of anger bubbling away inside their boiling blood. The anger exploded in their Revolution and they changed their world.

Eighty years after the 1789 Revolution the people rose up again – against their own government. And after that 1871 Communard Revolution the rebels were crushed with floods of blood and masses of cruelty. The days of watering the tree of liberty with blood were over.

The French have got rid of their kings and queens and emperors for good and put the guillotines away in museums. Hopefully they'll never have to get them out again.

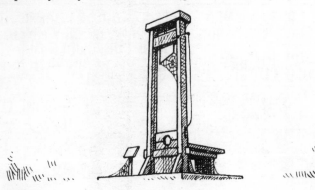